UNDERSTANDING
THE NATIONAL DEBT

UNDERSTANDING

THE

NATIONAL

DEBT

What Every American Needs to Know

CARL LANE

WESTHOLME
Yardley

Westholme Publishing, LLC
904 Edgewood Road
Yardley, Pennsylvania 19067
Visit our Web site at www.westholmepublishing.com

First Printing September 2016
10 9 8 7 6 5 4 3 2 1
ISBN: 978-1-59416-266-4
Also available in cloth and as an eBook.

Printed in the United States of America

For my grandsons,
Kaya, Han, and Kelly
And my grandnephew, Max
And the entire upcoming generation,
That they enjoy healthy and prosperous lives

CONTENTS

List of Tables

INTRODUCTION

History and Our Current National Debt

I N RECENT YEARS, AND ESPECIALLY NOW DURING THE 2016 presidential campaign, the news media and many politicians frequently remind us that the United States has a debt problem—namely, that the nation owes more than $19 trillion while its gross domestic product (GDP) is roughly only $18 trillion. Put another way, our national debt, we are told, is more than 100 percent of GDP, a debt-to-GDP ratio that is exceedingly unhealthy and unparalleled in our history since the end of World War II. Conservative Republicans perceive this debt as an immediate threat to our economy, a danger that is in our faces right now. Their solution is to espouse austerity, to cut federal expenditures to arrive at a balanced budget, and avoid becoming like Greece. Liberal Democrats, on the other hand, see the debt as a problem on a distant horizon, one to be addressed by increasing taxes, especially on the wealthiest elements in American society, to achieve a balanced budget.

These differences in perception and proposed solutions aim at the same target: a balanced federal budget. After all, eliminating annual budgetary deficits is the only way that the national debt can be pared down. Yet the Republican and Democratic alternatives have dominated debate about the debt issue for nearly a decade, and have stifled the emergence of new ideas which might transcend the austerity–versus–tax increase boundaries of the current discussion of the debt issue. The fate of the Bowles-Simpson (frequently called "Simpson–Bowles") Commission's report on "fiscal responsibility and reform" illustrates this point. It recommended both tax hikes and program cuts. Apparently for this reason, both conservative Republicans and liberal Democrats turned their backs on it. Although the report should have served as a springboard for negotiation and compromise, it was dead in the water upon publication.[1] This book constitutes an attempt to get beyond the "tax increase–program cuts" alternatives. It is an effort to confront the debt issue from outside of the proverbial box.

The debt is a problem for several reasons. For example, if the debt keeps mounting, creditors at some unknowable moment in the future may lose confidence that the United States can meet its payment obligations or worry that it will dilute the debt through currency inflation. In either case, creditors would demand higher interest rates or cease lending altogether. The result would be calamitous—severe economic depression or hyperinflation. Fortunately, at this moment neither of these scenarios seems likely.

Nonetheless, there is a more pressing problem. The more the government borrows, the less is available for private-sec-

---

1. *The Moment of Truth: Report of the National Commission on Fiscal Responsibility and Reform* (December 2010).

tor investment. This is the notorious "squeeze" effect. Increasing government debt "squeezes" out funds for corporate research and development, employee retraining, and other purposes. Put briefly, the "squeeze" inhibits economic growth.

Finally, the most immediately burdensome problem the debt presents to the nation is the interest due on it each year. The Congressional Budget Office (CBO) estimated that net interest on the debt in 2015 would equal 1.3 percent of our gross domestic product (GDP), which now stands at slightly more than $18 trillion.[2] Note that these interest payments represent substantial amounts of money. (See table I.1.)

Table I.1
Interest on the Gross National Debt, 2010–2015

2010	$413,954,825,362.17
2011	$454,393,280,417.03
2012	$359,796,008,919.49
2013	$415,688,781,248.40
2014	$430,812,121,372.05
2015	$402,435,356,075.49

(Source: www.treasurydirect.gov/govt/reports/ir/ir_ expense.htm.)

Most recently, in 2015, the Treasury Department paid more than $400 billion in interest on the national debt.[3] The point being that every dollar spent on interest is a dollar less for

2. Congressional Budget Office, "The 2015 Long-Term Budget Outlook," June 2015, 3.
3. "Interest Expense on the Debt Outstanding," www.treasurydirect.gov/ govt/reports/ir/ir_expense.htm.

other purposes. In other words, those elements of the federal budget deemed "discretionary" suffer. The mandatory elements of the budget—Social Security, Medicare, Medicaid, and the interest on the debt must be provided for, but defense and national security, education, energy, infrastructure repair and development, climate change, and other needs wind up with less. Just imagine for a moment a no-debt situation. No debt, of course, means no interest payments. If there had been no debt in fiscal year 2015, $402 billion would have been available to fund other needs. Interest on the national debt, in short, deprives us of money we could use for better purposes. This matter has acquired deeper urgency because, as was widely anticipated, the Federal Reserve raised interest rates in December 2015. Borrowing from the public has become more costly.

In any event, for all these reasons the national debt, whether a problem in our faces now or on the horizon, must sooner or later be addressed. Accordingly, it is essential to quantify its exact size. When the news media, elected officials, government bureaucrats, and various academics tell us that we confront a national debt greater than $19 trillion, they are technically correct—but only technically. Nineteen-trillion-plus is the gross national debt. Yet the gross debt conceals the fact that it is composed of two elements: the public debt and "intragovernment holdings."[4] The public debt consists of bonds, bills, and notes that investors purchase at the current market interest rate. Investors constitute diverse elements: domestic and foreign individuals, banks, insurance companies, hedge and retirement funds, foreign institutions and govern-

4. Bureau of the Fiscal Service, Department of the Treasury, "Daily Treasury Statement: Cash and Debt Operations of the United States Treasury."

ments, and college and university endowments, to name just a few. Those investments are secured not by congressional legislation but signed and sealed by contract with the US Treasury and backed by the "full faith and credit" of the United States. Payment of interest and principal is guaranteed according to the schedule defined in the contract between creditor and Treasury. Missing a scheduled interest or principal payment would constitute default. (The United States has never defaulted, and, if it did, the results would be calamitous for the world economy.) In any case, according to the Bureau of the Fiscal Service, on June 6, 2016, the public debt amounted to more than $13.8 trillion.[5]

The other element of the gross national debt, "intragovernment holdings," is what the government borrows from various trust funds that it has created over the years. While there are a number of such funds from which Treasury borrows annually, the principal in-house creditors are the Social Security and Medicare trust funds, especially the former. In other words, the term "intragovernment holdings" refers to money that the US Treasury borrows from other parts of the government at interest rates defined by law. The special-issue securities by which these loan transactions are accomplished are not marketable to the public; the borrowing and the interest payments are intragovernment transactions only. Briefly put, the government borrows from itself and pays interest to itself on these loans. On June 6, 2016, the Bureau of the Fiscal Service reported that the intragovernment holdings portion of the gross national debt totaled more than $5.3 trillion.[6] That amount, combined with the public debt, adds

5. Ibid. The precise total was $13,881,076,000,000.
6. Ibid. To be precise, the amount was $5,339,408,000,000.

up to the gross debt of more than $19 trillion.[7] Accordingly, in round numbers, the intragovernment holdings account for approximately 27.7 percent of the gross national debt. Yet that is money that we literally owe to *ourselves*. Does uniting that amount with the public debt in fact distort the reality of our debt situation? Probably, yes. Put another way: if we missed an interest payment to ourselves, would that constitute default? Probably not. Can we sue ourselves? Probably not. The Congressional Budget Office, it is worth noting, does not endorse or in any way promote the distortion that the combination of the public debt and the intragovernment holdings represents.[8] It separates the two, recognizing that the real debt challenge facing the United States is $13.8-trillion-plus, not $19.2-trillion-plus—about 74 percent of GDP, not more than 100 percent of GDP.[9] Much more remains to be said later about the intragovernment holdings. Suffice it to say at this point that their volume offers an opportunity to address our real debt challenge—principal and interest on the public debt—in a new and creative way.

The $13.8-trillion-plus debt owed to the public is obviously a lot of money. What to do about it has been the source of very deep and bitter partisan contention. Consensus is nowhere in sight. For this reason, it is useful and perhaps even comforting to recall that since gaining independence in 1776 the United States has been debt-free for only two years and ten months (from January 1835 to October 1837). We have lived with public debt for nearly all our national history. The only thing that makes the current debt seem so fearsome is its

7. Ibid. Again, to be precise, on June 6, 2016, the gross debt totaled $19,220,484,000,000.
8. See, for example, CBO's "The 2015 Long-Term Budget Outlook."
9. Ibid., title page and passim.

magnitude. Yet even that reality needs context. Today, the real debt-to-GDP ratio is approximately 74 percent. At the end of WWII it was well over 100 percent.[10] Yet no economic catastrophe ensued. Indeed, the post-WWII debt was pared down, albeit not eliminated, over the subsequent quarter century, coinciding with an era of unmatched prosperity.

For deeper historical context with respect to our current debt situation, it may be helpful to flashback to that one brief period, 1835–1837, when the United States was debt-free. How did the presidential administrations of Andrew Jackson secure debt extinction?[11] More important, does the Jacksonian experience in securing debt freedom offer us any guidance regarding our current debt problem? This is not an irrelevant question, even though nearly two centuries separate us from the Age of Jackson. To Jackson's generation, the debt ($127-million-plus) inherited from the War for Independence, the Louisiana Purchase, and the War of 1812 seemed, by the standards of the day, an insurmountable sum to pay off. In the early nineteenth century no one had ever seen 127 million of anything, in the same way that, today, few if any have ever seen 13 trillion of anything. Then, as now, such an amount was beyond imagination. But times, of course, have changed. Nowadays many CEOs of large corporations, professional athletes, stars in the entertainment industries, and others earn salaries that match and often exceed the post–War of 1812 national debt. From that perspective, we have more in common with the Jackson era than what is readily apparent.

10. Ibid., figure 1.1, 11.
11. For the answer to this question, see Carl Lane, *A Nation Wholly Free: The Elimination of the National Debt in the Age of Jackson* (Yardley, PA: Westholme Publishing, 2014).

If the Jacksonian experience with debt reduction and debt freedom has anything to offer us, it is guidance, not lessons. Why? Because history has no lessons to teach. If it does, our intellects are too feeble to grasp them. History simply tells us where we have been and how we got to where we are. Understanding these matters can give us some sense of direction into the unknowable future. History can serve as a "lantern," as the late and great American historian Allan Nevins once remarked, into the darkness of tomorrows to come.[12] Or, as Paolo Mauro of the International Monetary Fund has written:"Our belief is that although today's circumstances may be different from those experienced in the past, history may nevertheless provide useful guidance."[13]

I have told the story of how debt freedom was achieved in 1835 elsewhere, and that work has inspired this effort.[14] It aims at using the Jacksonian experience as Nevins's "lantern." Simply remembering that we once confronted an enormous debt and defeated it should inspire confidence that we can do it again; or, in one of today's colloquialisms,"been there, done that." With patience, wisdom, an appreciation of what the past has to offer, and, above all else, leadership that embodies those attributes, we can look forward to a future in which our children, grandchildren, and great grandchildren will enjoy prosperous lives.

Finally, it is important to note that the CBO's 2015 "Long-Term Budget Outlook" constituted a major source for much of the data cited here. Accordingly, that means some numbers

12. Allan Nevins, *The Gateway to History*, rev. ed. (New York: Anchor Books, 1962), 14.
13. Paolo Mauro, ed., *Chipping Away at Public Debt: Sources of Failure and Keys to Success in Fiscal Adjustment* (Hoboken, NJ: Wiley, 2011), xv.
14. Lane, *A Nation Wholly Free.*

may change when the Budget Office issues its next report in June 2016. Nonetheless, the ideas presented here to achieve pathways to a balanced budget that transcend the limitations of either austerity or tax increases may still enlighten us. We need new thinking on the debt question, and, hopefully, this work will contribute to the national debate.

ECONOMIC GROWTH AND THE PUBLIC DEBT

EALING SUCCESSFULLY WITH OUR NATIONAL DEBT REQUIRES paring back annual budgetary deficits until they reach zero or better—a balanced budget or surplus revenue. This is obvious because the debt is the sum of previous deficits. A budget in balance or a revenue surplus means that borrowing becomes unnecessary. Accordingly, the debt then shrinks as obligations mature and principal is returned to the lender. Interest payments on redeemed bonds, of course, cease. Result: the national debt begins to wind down. For this reason, balancing the budget, if not generating surplus revenue, should be one of the main targets of public policy, whether short- or long-term. What is the status of our annual budgetary deficits now? The answer to that question constitutes both good and bad news. The good news is that in FY 2013 the deficit amounted to just over $719 billion but in 2014 had diminished to a little more than $514 billion.[1] According to the CBO, the deficit in FY 2015 amounted to about $420 billion.[2] In other words, over fiscal years 2013–15 significant progress had been made against the deficit. In fact, in July 2015 *The Wall Street Journal* touted the news that we were "digging out" of recurring annual deficits.[3] The bad news is that CBO anticipates a deficit in FY 2016 of about $534 billion, an increase of more than $100 billion over 2015.[4] If that estimate is correct, then we have failed to keep deficit reduction on track toward zero. This unfortunate circumstance is likely the result of inadequate economic growth in the wake of the 2008 Great Recession.

Economic growth is the key to keeping us on track to ongoing debt reduction. What is economic growth? It is the increase in per capita production in a given year, and the total output in goods and services in a given year (gross domestic product, or GDP) measures the size of the economy. Without growth in GDP, tackling the debt problem will resemble Don Quixote's tilting with windmills.

History offers some "lantern" light on this matter. The two decades following the War of 1812, culminating in the complete elimination of the national debt in 1835, illustrate the importance of a growing economy in dealing with debt. In

1. White House, Office of Management and Budget: Historical Tables, table 1.1, "Summary of Receipts, Outlays, and Surpluses or Deficits, 1789–2020."
2. CBO, www.cbo.gov/topics/budget.
3. Nick Timiraos, "US Annual Budget Deficit Remains Near Seven-Year Low in June," *Wall Street Journal*, July 13, 2015.
4. CBO, Report, "Updated Budget Projections: 2016–2026," March 24, 2016, www.cbo.gov/topics/budget.

1815, the first full year of peace after the war against Great Britain, GDP amounted to approximately $930 million.[5] That volume shrank in the wake of the Panic of 1819 and the ensuing recession. By 1825, however, GDP was growing again, and by 1828, the year of Andrew Jackson's election to the presidency, it had recovered to $897 million.[6] Subsequently, GDP grew every year.

Table 1.1
The United States GDP, 1829–1835

Year	Nominal GDP in millions[7]
1829	$930
1830	$1,022
1831	$1,052
1832	$1,129
1833	$1,158
1834	$1,219
1835	$1,340 (debt freedom year)

Growth in GDP provided the government sufficient surpluses to discharge the national debt fully. Why? Because the growth meant prosperity, and Americans possessed the wherewithal to buy imported products and pay the tariff duties on them. At that time, duties on imports were the primary source of federal revenues.

As GDP grew, so too did the American population, both from natural increase and from immigration. In 1828, when Jackson was elected, the population of the United States

5. Louis Johnston and Samuel H. Williamson, "What Was the US GDP Then?," *MeasuringWorth*, 2015.
6. Ibid.
7. Ibid.

stood at approximately 12.24 million; by 1835, the debt-freedom year, it had risen to roughly fifteen million.[8] In other words, as the economy grew and the population increased, the size of the national debt, per capita, declined to zero.

What accounted for GDP growth in Jackson's era? There is no simple answer to that question. Rather, a number of circumstances explain it. Population growth, both free and slave, constitutes one factor. More people were producing more goods and services. The concurrent prosperity, as already mentioned, allowed more and more Americans to buy imported goods and pay the import duties on them, filling the coffers of the federal Treasury. In addition, American westward expansion brought more and more new land under cultivation. Agricultural production increased, and the sale of public lands in the West increasingly contributed to the national Treasury. Canal and turnpike construction, followed by railroad development, created an ever-widening domestic market. Lastly, the Second Bank of the United States provided—until it died at the hands of Andrew Jackson in 1836—stability to the American economy; that is, currency inflation remained in check. Elimination of the national debt in 1835 seemed like sweet icing on top of all this.

———

Our national economy today is, of course, very different from that in Jackson's day. In that era the United States was predominantly agricultural. Most Americans made their living from farming, whether to produce cereal grains, dairy goods, or exportable commodities like slave-produced cotton and tobacco. American society was, in other words, largely rural.

8. US Bureau of the Census, *Historical Statistics of the United States, Colonial Times to 1957* (Washington, DC: Government Printing Office, 1960), 7.

Nonetheless, beginning around 1840, manufacturing began to account for larger and larger shares of GDP, and the era following the Civil War witnessed a fully blown industrial revolution. The factory system promoted increased urbanization, and, by about 1920, most Americans were living in cities. Immigrants from overseas, millions arriving in the period from 1880 to 1924, provided much of the labor to sustain industrialization. New energy sources played a major role as well: oil, coal, and electricity quickly displaced waterpower to keep American factories humming. Technological advances rapidly put new products on the market—automobiles, radios, telephones, refrigerators, vacuum cleaners, and toasters, to mention just a few. To assist manufacturers in marketing these new products, an entirely new industry emerged—advertising (a.k.a. "Madison Avenue"). Its role was to persuade Americans to buy particular products, whether they needed them or not. Since at least the 1920s, if not earlier, consumerism has driven the American economy. Put differently, consumption accounts for the vitality and health of our economy. As long as Americans purchase the goods and services the economy generates, all is well. Supply and demand are in rough balance, and all benefit. Producers enjoy their profits, and consumers enjoy what they have bought. Every able-bodied man and woman is productive. Unemployment is low. Salaries and wages are adequate enough to assure that workers continue to consume, and they, of course, pay taxes on their incomes to allow government to do the things it needs to do. As GDP grows, Treasury Department revenues grow. These circumstances were true in the Age of Jackson, and they remain true today, despite the enormous differences between the economy of the 1830s and that of the present. A growing economy improves the overall quality of life and, in the process, reduces public indebtedness. Accordingly, it would be extraordinarily helpful to know in advance how much the economy will grow, or *not* grow, in the immediate future.

Yet predicting the rate of annual economic growth (or decline) is a risky business. Economics, after all, is not a precise science. Nonetheless, nowadays many in that discipline doubt that the United States economy will grow at a rate that can impose downward pressure on the annual budgetary deficit and achieve balance between revenues and expenditures, a necessary first step toward debt reduction. The June 2015 CBO report, for example, paints a dismal future. "Economic growth will be slower in the future than it has been in the past. . . . CBO projects that real (inflation-adjusted) GDP will increase at an average annual rate of 2.2 percent over the next 25 years, compared with 3.3 percent during the 1965–2007 period."[9] An inadequate growth rate, the entire report suggests, will render us unable to eliminate annual budgetary deficits and trim back the public debt.[10]

While this must be a source of concern, it is, at the same time, worth remembering that grim economic predictions in the past have sometimes proven false. They are then simply and totally forgotten. For example, long before the Great Recession of 2008, many prominent economists questioned the health of American economic growth. Indeed, it constituted a prime topic of discussion at the Bill Clinton/Al Gore economic conference in December 1992, weeks before Clinton and Gore were sworn into office. Michael Porter of the Harvard Business School told the Little Rock gathering that American economic growth was in deep jeopardy,

9. CBO, "The 2015 Long-Term Budget Outlook," 18.
10. Ibid. and passim.

because the private sector did not invest enough in research and development and retraining the work force. "If we cannot change this state of affairs . . . our companies are going to lose market position, we're not going to grow productivity, we're not going to grow our economy, and we're not going to create jobs."[11] John White, then the director of the Center for Business and Government at the Harvard Kennedy School of Government, spoke at the same conference, focusing on the annual federal budgetary deficits. He told President-Elect Clinton that our "huge federal deficit . . . is a specific drag on our ability to have the kind of [economic] growth that we all desire."[12] He went on to predict that deficits would deepen and impede growth over the subsequent decade.[13] As is well known, however, such prognostications proved far from the mark, and hardly anyone remembers them anymore. Vibrant economic growth characterized the Clinton years;[14] an extraordinary outburst of creativity in the technology field accounted for much of the progress. New companies emerged and thrived, full employment was realized, and increased government revenues ultimately eliminated the deficits. In 2000 and 2001, the Treasury reported surpluses for the first time in a very long time. Suddenly many in government, business, and academia were predicting debt freedom by the second decade of the twenty-first century. Another Jackson-like 1835 seemed upon the short horizon.[15]

11. President Clinton's "New Beginning: The Complete Text," December 14–15, 1992, 43.
12. Ibid., 48.
13. Ibid., 48–55.
14. The average annual growth rate was 3.58 percent. "Presidents and Prosperity: The Underlying Data," *Forbes*, www.forbes.com2004/07/20/cx_da_0720presidentstable.html.
15. Lane, *A Nation Wholly Free*, 204–8.

Predicting the future is not only hazardous for economists but for historians as well, and for anyone in the imprecise social sciences. When George W. Bush became president in January 2001, with a tax-cutting agenda, who could have predicted the 9/11 attacks? The ensuing war in Afghanistan, the 2003 invasion of Iraq, and the drawn-out conflict there, together with the tax cuts, reinstituted deficit spending. When Bush left office in early 2009, the gross national debt had soared to $10.025 trillion, or 68 percent of GDP.

The onset of the Great Recession at the end of 2008 deeply complicated the financial problem. Bear Sterns and Lehman Brothers crashed. AIG, the huge insurance firm, teetered on the edge of bankruptcy, as did the automotive giants GM and Chrysler. Other businesses collapsed. Credit markets froze. Workers lost their jobs. Fear tightened its fist on the economy. In its final weeks, the Bush administration began bailing out banks and businesses "too big to fail" but not others. The economy seemed headed for a rerun of the 1930s.

All these problems confronted the incoming Obama administration with challenges unmatched since the inauguration of Franklin Roosevelt in 1933. With little alternative, Obama also pursued bailouts, particularly in the auto industry. In addition, in 2009 he secured from Congress the American Recovery and Reinvestment Act, commonly called the "stimulus," which aimed at injecting money into infrastructure repair and development, education, state and local government coffers, and other causes in order to create and to preserve jobs. The stimulus amounted to $787 billion, but more than one-third of it ($285.6 billion) constituted temporary payroll tax relief to increase the disposable income of the greatest number of people. The administration hoped that people would spend the tax savings and that increased consumer demand would promote economic recovery.

Bailouts and stimulus, of course, grew the national debt, but rapid recovery did not ensue. Economic growth flattened out, and the gross national debt rose to where it is today—more than 100 percent of GDP, an amount trumpeted to us on an almost daily basis. (Keep in mind that the debt to the public, the portion of the debt we do not owe to ourselves, is actually about 74 percent of GDP.)

Why? The short answer is probably obvious. The recession caused federal revenues to fall. The millions who lost their jobs ceased paying income taxes. Instead of contributing to the national Treasury, they filed for and collected unemployment insurance, which, of course, was their right. But depending on unemployment insurance hardly constitutes affluence. It promotes anxiety about the future. How long will it take to get another job? Will I ever be offered another job? Can unemployment insurance meet all my needs? Rent? Mortgage payments? Energy bills? Groceries? Medical needs? These worries resulted in predictable behavior. Unemployment compensation, especially for those living from paycheck to paycheck, left little, if any, disposable income, and those who found themselves in this uncomfortable predicament did the wise thing. They simply did not make the purchases they would have made had they not lost their jobs. The new computer will have to wait; so, too, will the new suit or dress; the kids' sneakers will have to do a little longer. Put simply, those who lost their jobs ceased to be robust participants in our consumption-driven economy, and, at the same time, unemployment compensation imposed a further burden on government revenue.

The problem did not end there. Those who were fortunate enough to retain their jobs worried that another round of layoffs could pull them into the ranks of the unemployed. Job insecurity led them to cut back on purchases as the already unemployed had done. Anticipating the dreaded "pink slip," they postponed buying a new car, stopped eating out on Saturday nights, and simply eliminated unnecessary expenditures until the fear cloud fled. Fear prolonged the recession, and even at this late date we are not 100 percent recovered. (Joblessness, for example, remains a problem in the Rust Belt and in Appalachia.)

The rate of consumption of the goods and services the economy generates is one measure of economic health. A decline in consumption hurts. Businesses, unable to sell what they have produced, reduce their work force in order to remain profitable. Yet every termination reduces consumption and deepens the deflation into which the economy slides. In such an environment business and investor communities, especially banks, are exceedingly reluctant to extend credit or loans. This is what the Great Recession was all about. In 2009 and beyond, fear gripped both labor and capital, and in the past it has often been very difficult to break that mindset. Franklin Roosevelt put his finger directly on this problem when he said, in his first inaugural address, at the deepest moment of the Great Depression: "The only thing we have to fear is fear itself."

Fear does not promote economic growth. Robust consumption does. For this reason, *increasing the disposable income of the greatest number of families should be one of the great objects of public policy*. Strong annual economic growth—3 percent–plus—is essential to closing the budgetary deficits, shrinking the obligatory interest obligations the government faces every year, and generating the surpluses that will pare back the national debt. Vigorous economic growth in Andrew Jackson's time, as we have seen, provided the context for elimination of the national debt in 1835.

Increasing the disposable income of the greatest number of families entails an overhaul of our present tax system. Presently, as is well known, the structure favors the wealthiest 1.0 percent of taxpayers. The justification rests on the idea that these favored few—less than one-and-a-half-million taxpayers out of a total 136 million—will devote their tax savings to investment in theirs and other business enterprises and, as a result, create jobs and promote the general welfare.[16] We often refer to this rationale as "trickle-down," or "dribble-down," theory. It became the foundation of the 1924 tax overhaul advocated by then–Secretary of the Treasury Andrew Mellon, passed by Congress, and signed into law by President Calvin Coolidge. Yet the wealthy beneficiaries of the tax law seem to have found other things to do with the money they saved in taxes, like long and lavish vacations in Europe or throwing money into the accounts of brokerage firms during the great bull market of the 1920s, to mention two. In other words, much, if not most, of these tax savings among the wealthiest American families were not deployed for productivity. Trickle-down not only failed but also became one of the several causes of the Great Depression. Trickle-down, in fact, has never worked. Pinning hopes on it today to foster economic growth is unlikely to have a positive outcome.

Trickle-down economics has had a poor track record for reasons that go beyond simple self-indulgence, greed, and other human failings. The top 1.0 percent of income earners are too few to carry an economy the size of the United

16. Tax Foundation, "Summary of Latest Federal Income Tax Data," 2012. The uppermost 1.0 percent constitutes less than 1 percent of all taxpayers. In 2012, their average adjusted gross income amounted to $1,976,738.

States. Whatever the size and scope of their investment activities, their numbers are too small, regardless of their wealth, to exert sufficient demand on an $18 trillion economy in a recession. Even the richest of the rich limit the number of houses they own, the automobiles they possess, the refrigerators in their kitchens, the televisions in their dens, the computers in their home offices, and the clothes washers and driers in their basements. This list can easily be extended. The point is this: the actual purchasing power of the wealthiest 1.0 percent in the United States cannot come close to matching mass consumption. Simply put, the 1.0 percent cannot grow the economy.

Increasing the disposable income of the greatest number of families, however, does grow the economy. We know what needs to be done to maximize the purchasing power of more and more families. More must be spent on infrastructure repair and development, education, job retraining, and research and development. All this, of course, entails greater government expenditures and running up the public debt even further, at least initially. But as more and more jobs are created and filled, the more government tax revenues will increase, and the less government will pay out in unemployment insurance and other safety-net obligations like food stamps and Medicaid. Put another way, as employment increases, more and more families acquire disposable income, and many, if not most, will spend it on things they have wanted but postponed buying. Demand for goods and services will rise, and American agriculture, manufacturing, and service industries will do what they need to do to satisfy that demand. After all, that's how they harvest profits. Stimulating strong economic growth sounds easy, but achieving it has not been.

Why not? Because there remains another very important related matter, a problem that is very much in the news nowadays and which constitutes an obstacle, if not a contradiction, to the seemingly easy restoration of healthy economic growth through job creation. That problem is the ever-increasing inequality of income in the United States. The more wealth flows to the uppermost percentile, the less wealth remains for the other 99 percent to share. This reality serves to undermine the capacity of most American families to acquire the kind of disposable income that would generate vigorous economic growth. Indeed, it is one of the factors that has prevented a more rapid recovery from the Great Recession. Capital's capacity to acquire wealth at the expense of labor stifles growth.

Thomas Piketty's recent and trenchant *Capital in the Twenty-First Century* addressed this matter head-on. His fundamental thesis is that if the rate of return on capital is greater than the rate of economic growth, then wealth will flow to those with the greatest amount of capital.[17] In effect, the distribution of wealth becomes skewed in favor of those with assets that generate income without work (stocks, bonds, rental properties, etc.).[18] Anyone who has ever played the board game *Monopoly* understands how this works.[19] Players with properties on the two sides of the board before "Go," especially Park Place and Boardwalk, and who build houses and then hotels on them, wind up accumulating more and more of their opponents' cash. The latter are ultimately forced

17. Thomas Piketty, *Capital in the Twenty-First Century*, trans. Arthur Goldhammer (Cambridge, MA: Harvard University Press, 2014), 25.
18. Ibid., 233–34.
19. Reference here is to the classic Atlantic City version.

to sell whatever assets they may have acquired along the way, and the two-hundred-dollar reward for passing "Go" hardly suffices to keep them in the game. Meaning? The losers lose because their disposable income keeps shrinking until it reaches zero. Why does their disposable income keep shrinking? Because in *Monopoly* there is no such thing as economic growth: the money supply is fixed and cannot expand; the properties on the board are also finite, as are the number of houses and hotels that may be built. Since economic growth is an impossibility within the game, wealth rapidly flows to the player or players with the most valuable assets.

Piketty maintains that in the United States today (but not only in the US) the rate of return on capital exceeds that of economic growth with the same consequences as in *Monopoly*. "Since 1980," he writes, "income inequality has exploded in the United States. The upper decile's share increased from 30–35 percent of national income in the 1970s to 45–50 percent in the 2000s—an increase of 15 points of national income."[20] This reality undermines economic growth's capacity to solve our deficit and debt problems. As greater and greater shares of national wealth drift to fewer and fewer families, then the disposable income of all other families shrinks. It is important to note that this circumstance did not exist in the era of Andrew Jackson. Piketty points out that a "low capital/income ratio" characterized the American economy in the first several decades under the Constitution.[21] Accordingly, it was easier for the Jacksonians to discharge the national debt because their economy was not driven by mass consumption—and because labor, not capital, was generating national income.

20. Piketty, *Capital in the Twenty-First Century*, 294.
21. Ibid., 152.

Everything that can be done to promote economic growth must be done. Many policies and policy proposals are in action or under discussion to increase goods and services: build and/or repair infrastructure; promote education and job retraining, especially through community colleges; elevate the minimum wage and overtime compensation; extend unemployment benefits to those who still need them; invest in research and development. All these efforts, taken together, will narrow the gap between (*r*) the rate of return on capital and (*g*) the rate of economic growth. As Piketty has demonstrated, when *r* is greater than *g*, national wealth flows upward to the few, leaving the majority with smaller and smaller shares of national income and less disposable resources with which to engage fully in the consumer economy.[22] Reversing Piketty's formulation so that *g* is greater than *r* would recreate the kind of economic environment that prevailed when Andrew Jackson led the nation to debt freedom. Achieving that objective will not be easy. In fact, it constitutes an extraordinary challenge. After all, today our rate of economic growth (*g*) stands at about 2.2 percent per year, while the rate of return on capital (*r*) is much higher than that.[23]

Accordingly, we need to get deficit shrinkage back on track. The less we borrow from the public and the less we pay in interest, the more there will be available for national security, education, infrastructure, and other discretionary matters. All these aid economic growth, but not fast enough to get us quickly to a balanced budget and ultimate surpluses. Policy initiatives suggested by the Jacksonian era of debt freedom, however, can accelerate the elimination of the annual deficits—but these have thus far been overlooked, because

22. Ibid., 25.
23. Ibid., 347–50.

discussion of the issue has been bounded by the retrenchment–versus–tax increase debate.

2

POSTPONING INTEREST PAYMENTS ON THE INTRAGOVERNMENTAL DEBT

EMBEDDED IN THE OTHERWISE GLOOMY 2015 CBO BUDGET report are a few scraps of good news. One of them is that "federal revenues as a share of GDP are projected to rise from 17.7 percent of GDP in 2015 to 18.3 percent in 2025." Indeed, according to CBO, after 2025 "revenues continue rising faster than GDP."[1] Result? By 2040, revenues will constitute 19.4 percent of GDP.[2] The main reason for this growth is "bracket creep—the pushing of a growing share of income into higher tax brackets."[3] Increasing federal revenues obviously generate opportunity to pare back deficits. *Carpe diem.* Now is the time to act.

---

1. CBO, "The 2015 Long-Term Budget Outlook," 63. CBO dismisses the importance of increased revenues on the ground that expenditures will grow at a faster rate.
2. Ibid., 63–64.
3. Ibid., 63.

Vigorous economic growth, it will be recalled, is the key to deficit and ultimately debt reduction, and vigorous economic growth depends in large measure upon maximizing the disposable income of the greatest number of families. Yet today economic growth hovers at about 2.2 percent, a rate inadequate to invert Piketty's dictum that when r is greater than g, wealth is skewed to fewer and fewer families among the uppermost 1 percent of income earners.[4]

Complicating matters is the fact that the workforce is shrinking. Fewer and fewer people are contributing to GDP. One reason is that the fertility rate in the United States is quite low. Relying on data provided by the Social Security Administration, CBO projects "an average fertility rate of 2.0 children per woman between 2015 and 2040."[5] This demographic reality makes job creation easier because fewer people will need them. Yet a low birth rate is not the only reason for a shrinking workforce. Another is that the baby boom generation is now retiring. This circumstance not only affects American productivity but also the condition of the social safety net—Social Security, Medicare, Medicaid, and now Obamacare. Because of improvements in modern medicine and the widespread adoption of healthful living habits, retirees are living longer and longer. Senior citizens, in other words, are becoming an ever-larger percentage of the total population. CBO projects the "US population will increase from 325 million at the beginning of 2015 to 394 million in 2040."[6] Currently, those over the age of sixty-five constitute about 25 percent of the population. By 2025, they will account for approximately 33 percent, and by 2040 about 39

4. CBO, "The 2015 Long-Term Budget Outlook," 18.
5. Ibid., appendix A, 111.
6. Ibid.

percent.[7] As they become an ever-larger segment of society, seniors must remain active participants in our consumer-driven economy in order to secure and sustain vibrant economic growth. This fact alone underscores the importance of Social Security to the well-being not only of senior citizens but also the entire nation. Put another way, maintaining and, better yet, increasing the disposable income of this rapidly growing element in American society is essential to national prosperity.

No social safety net programs like Social Security or Medicare existed in the Age of Jackson. Indeed, the only "entitlement" that existed, then as today, was interest and principal payments to the holders of the public debt. This benefit is very different from Social Security and other elements of today's safety net. The latter, created by acts of Congress, can be amended—even repealed. But interest and principal payments on the public debt are written into contracts between the creditor and the US Treasury. The "full faith and credit of the United States" guarantee fulfillment of these contracts, and a large body of contract law upholds the integrity of these agreements.

Nonetheless, many, if not most, Americans consider the laws that created the social safety net as "entitlements." Indeed, we, our politicians, the media—virtually everyone—commonly refer to them as "entitlements," and with good reason. After all, Americans have been paying payroll taxes into the safety net programs all their working lives, and feel entitled to the benefits for which they have paid. Keeping faith with the American people on these matters is one of the major obligations, both moral and legal, which government

7. Ibid., figure 3–2, 52.

faces. In addition, prosperity depends upon it, because the safety net has to do with the disposable income of a large and growing sector of the population.

Let's focus on Social Security. Created in 1935, it provides retirement benefits and unemployment and disability insurance. Almost all the program's funding—96 percent in 2015—derives from the payroll tax, which amounts to 12.4 percent on earnings. Employers and employees share the burden—or 6.2 percent each. The payroll taxes are credited to the Social Security trust fund, which is made up of two legally separate entities, Old Age and Survivors Insurance (OASI) and Disability Insurance (DI).[8] In 2014 combined, OASDI revenue from the payroll tax amounted to $756 billion.[9] The remaining four percent of income to the system comes from modifications to the original Social Security Act that, under certain circumstances, tax the benefits themselves. Beneficiaries with other income pay tax on their Social Security benefits when their adjusted gross income and half their retirement benefits are greater than $25,000 for single tax filers, or $32,000 for joint filers.[10] This tax on benefits raises a substantial amount of money. In 2014, for example, it generated approximately $28 billion to OASI and roughly $1.7 billion to DI.[11] The total, about $29.7 billion, equaled three percent of OASDI revenues that year.[12] Total tax revenue to the Social Security trust funds in 2014 was $785.6 billion. At the same time, total outlay for benefits amounted

8. CBO, "The 2015 Long-Term Budget Outlook," 51.
9. 2015 OASDI Trustees Report, table II.B1, "Summary of 2014 Trust Fund Financial Operations."
10. CBO, "The 2015 Long-Term Budget Outlook," 51.
11. 2015 OASDI Trustees Report, table II.B1, "Summary of 2014 Trust Fund Financial Operations."
12. Ibid.

to $848.5 billion.[13] In other words, benefit payments exceeded tax revenues by roughly $58.8 billion. Ordinarily, one would think that this deficit would leave the trust funds swimming in red ink, but no—at the end of 2014 the balance (or asset reserves) in the trust funds was $2.7895 billion.[14] Remarkable! Even more remarkable is the fact that this represented an increase over the balance at the end of 2013, which was $2.7644 billion.[15] Accordingly, even though benefit payments were greater than payroll and benefit tax revenues in 2014, the Social Security trust funds improved their assets by $25.1 billion.

How could this be? The answer is that the payroll tax and the tax on benefits are not the only sources of Social Security revenue. Under legislation enacted in the 1970s, surpluses in government-sponsored trust funds (there are others besides OASI and DI) must be loaned to the Treasury. These loans are the "intragovernment holdings." For about a quarter century before the baby boomers began retiring, OASI and DI ran surpluses and invested them, as law required, in special, non-marketable government bonds called special-issue securities. These loans were not, nor are they today, interest-free. Rather, by law, the interest rate for these non-marketable securities must match "the average market yield, as of the last business day of the prior month."[16] If and whenever OASI or DI needs cash "to meet current operating expenses," the law authorizes Treasury to redeem "at par value" the amount that

13. Ibid. The deficit stemmed from the payroll tax relief built into the 2009 stimulus.
14. Ibid.
15. Ibid.
16. Ibid., appendices, 2; CBO, "The 2015 Long-Term Budget Outlook," 51.

will allow the trust funds to meet their obligations.[17] This process, in fact, covered the 2014 gap between Social Security revenues and benefit payments.[18]

All this may seem complicated, but it is not. It simply means that the Department of Treasury borrows from the Social Security Trust Funds to help finance government operations and to thereby reduce the amount borrowed from the public. This practice, therefore, constitutes a deficit-reduction measure. In return for the loans, Treasury issues special short-term certificates of indebtedness and long-term bonds, in effect IOUs, at a rate of interest defined by law. Government, in brief, borrows from itself. The special-issue securities held by OASDI are a major element of their assets. They represent, as we have seen, no small amount. In 2014 these holdings were well over $2 trillion, and the interest Treasury paid to OASDI that year amounted to more than $98 billion, or about 11 percent of total OASDI revenue.[19] So, specifically, how much has Treasury borrowed from OASDI, and at what interest rates, since 2010? (See table 2.1.)

How does any of this relate to Andrew Jackson's era? There were no Social Security trust funds in his day and age. Moreover, a booming economy allowed him to pursue retrenchment as the principal mechanism to pare down the national debt until it reached zero in 1835. On the surface it seems that little comparison exists between Jackson's time and

17. 2015 OASIDI Trustees Report, appendices, 2.
18. Ibid., table II.B1.
19. Social Security and Medicare Boards of Trustees, "Status of the Social Security and Medicare Programs: A Summary of the 2015 Annual Reports," 8, 22.

Table 2.1

Treasury Loans from OASDI and Average Annual Interest Rates, 2010–2015

Fiscal Year	OASDI Acquisitions of Special-Issue Securities Average Annual (in thousands)	Interest Rate
2010	$1,019,839,317	2.760 percent
2011	$1,015,308,728	2.417 percent
2012	$1,065,659,757	1.458 percent
2013	$1,065,406,972	1.875 percent
2014	$1,083,901,789	2.271 percent
2015	$951,095,918	2.250 percent

(Sources: Social Security Administration Online: "Trust Fund Data, Investment Transactions," www.ssa.gov/cgi-bin/transactions.cgi; ibid., "Nominal Interest Rates on Special Issues," www.ssa.gov/oact/pro gdata/newIssue Rates.html.)

ours. Yet at least one parallel may be drawn between the Age of Jackson and ours concerning the interest payments on the intragovernment holdings.

First of all, Andrew Jackson would very likely have looked askance at one element of the government borrowing from another. Government departments and subordinate units lived within the budgetary allocations Congress provided. Government was much simpler then. But despite whatever reservations he would have had if such a situation had emerged during his presidency, he would have acquiesced, grudgingly for sure, but acquiesced nonetheless, because the alternative—borrowing from the public—was the greater evil. Yet Jackson would have been astonished that one element of government, borrowing from another, paid interest on the loan. He might very well have drawn the line on that point. This scenario is, of course, hypothetical but not entirely counterfactual. One of the major issues confronting his administrations bears on this matter: the question of the public lands.

During the Confederation era (1781–1788), all the states that had claims to territory in what was then "the West" (trans-Appalachia to the Mississippi River) ceded those claims to the United States to serve as a "common fund" for all the states, both then and in the future. Under the Constitution, ratified in 1788, those cessions remained legally binding upon the new federal government, and in 1790 Congress legislated that money raised from the sale of those lands was to be dedicated to reducing the national debt. No special fund was created to do this. All federal revenues, regardless of source, were simply mixed together at Treasury.[20]

When Jackson became president, national debt freedom was on the short horizon. The dedication of public land-sale revenues to debt extinction would shortly become obsolescent. Indeed, Treasury surpluses were likely. What was to be done? In 1833, Senator Henry Clay of Kentucky proposed legislation to distribute such revenue to the states, offering in his plan a 10 percent rebate to the states in which the land was located before the general distribution began. Congress passed the Clay bill, but Jackson pocket-vetoed it.[21]

Jackson explained his reasons for the veto when Congress met in its next session. In addition to other factors, Jackson rejected the 10 percent rebate, which accounted for one-

20. Lane, *A Nation Wholly Free*, 146–50.
21. Ibid., 151.

eighth of the revenues, leaving only seven-eighths for all the states, including rebate recipients, to share. That provision, he asserted, violated the original cession agreements of the 1780s. In effect, the states without federal landholdings would be paying the western states that did something resembling interest on the sales. Jackson simply rejected the proposed rebate as illegal.[22]

Jackson also complained, it is worth noting, that the Clay proposal changed the longstanding system of combining at Treasury all federal revenues regardless of source. Clay's bill, he argued, would create a special fund whose balance would swell the sum to be distributed. The states, of course, would welcome this perpetuated, not incidental, surplus because its distribution would reduce their need to tax themselves. Consolidation of the states under federal dominance would result. Therefore, a special fund for the surplus threatened the constitutional division of powers between federal and state authorities and, for that reason, was unconstitutional. "Money is power," he said.[23]

———

Many politicians, journalists, government experts, and others maintain that the Social Security trust fund is heading toward insolvency. CBO holds that "the combined OASDI trust funds" will be "exhausted" in 2029, while the trustees of the OASI fund predict that it will be depleted in 2035.[24] The reality is that the Social Security trust fund is not going broke

22. Ibid., 153.
23. Ibid., 155.
24. CBO, "The 2015 Long-Term Budget Outlook," 55; "2015 OASDI Trustees Report," section II, overview, 1, www.ssa.gov/oact/tr/2015/II_A_highlights.html.

any time soon.[25] Its asset reserves are enormous. (See table 2.2.) The trust fund is awash in money. Social Security's net revenue inflow exceeds its net revenue outflow.

Table 2.2
OASDI Asset Reserves, 2010–2015
(In Trillions)

2010	$2.608,950
2011	$2.677,925
2012	$2.732,334
2013	$2.764,431
2014	$2.789,476
2015	$2.812,476

(Source: Social Security Administration; Bulletin, vol. 75, no. 1, chart 2: www.ssa.gov/OACT/STATS/table4a3.html.)

It is time to recall Andrew Jackson's observation that "money is power." He was right, of course. Money has the power to do many things. It very obviously has the power to shrink the annual budgetary deficits. Moreover, if Jackson had reservations about the propriety of intragovernment borrowing and, especially, the payment of interest on such loans, what guidance do his views have to offer? More to the point, how much did Treasury pay in interest to OASDI over, say,

25. Both CBO and the Social Security Administration predict that DI will run out of funds in 2017, but that is because OASI and DI are not legally linked as one entity. Congress will have to bail DI out. The simplest way to do it would be to pass legislation combining the two funds as one. OASI's overflowing coffer will resolve DI's difficulty. CBO, "The 2015 Long-Term Budget Outlook," 55; Social Security and Medicare Boards of Trustees, "Status of the Social Security and Medicare Programs: A Summary of the 2015 Annual Reports," 1–2.

the last six years, and what were the budgetary deficits in those years? What percentage of the deficits did the interest payments represent?[26] (See table 2.3.)

What do these numbers mean? What, if anything, do they suggest? First, it is important to remember that the amounts of the loans are substantial. (See table 2.1.) Treasury does not have to borrow equivalent sums from the public. Accordingly, the intragovernment holdings help reduce the $13.8-trillion-plus public debt. As Paul N. Van de Water, senior fellow at the Center on Budget and Policy Priorities, has pointed out, "when . . . the budget is in deficit, a Social Security cash surplus allows the government to borrow less from the public to finance the deficit. . . . After all, why should the Treasury borrow funds when it has cash in the till?"[27] The special-issue securities narrow the gap between revenues and expenditures. In fact, by doing so, they realize a goal dating all the way back to 1938. That year the "first Advisory Council on Social Security" wrote: "As long as the budget is not balanced, the net result [of issuing the Special Issue Securities] is to reduce the amounts which the Government has to borrow from banks, insurance companies and other private parties. When the budget is balanced, these moneys will be available for the reduction of the national debt held by the public."[28] At the same time, of course, the net interest on the special-issue securities serves to shift the burden of interest from the public debt to the debt that we owe to ourselves.

---

26. See CBO at www.cbo.gov/topics/budget.
27. Paul N. Van de Water, "Understanding the Social Security Trust Funds," Center on Budget and Policy Priorities, August 18, 2014, 1.
28. Ibid., 3.

Table 2.3
Interest Due to OASDI and Budgetary Deficits, 2010–2015
(In Millions)

Fiscal Year	Interest Due to OASDI	Budgetary Deficit	Percentage★
2010	$117,498	$1,294,373	9.0
2011	$114,355	$1,299,593	8.7
2012	$109,143	$1,086,963	10.0
2013	$102,820	$679,544	15.1
2014	$98,204	$484,602	20.2
2015	$93,300	$438,406	44

★Note that the percentages listed are not precisely accurate because the interest payments are accounted by the calendar year, ending December 31, while the deficits are accounted by the fiscal year, which ends every September 30.
(Sources: Social Security and Medicare Boards of Trustees, *A Summary of the 2016 Annual Reports*. For the deficits, see the White House's Office of Management and Budget at www.whitehouse.gov/omb/budget/historicals, Budget Summary of Receipts, Outlays, and Surpluses and Deficits, 1789–2021, table 1.1. For the interest payments, visit the Social Security Administration at http://ssa.gov/OACT/STATS/table4a3html #income.)

All this is well and good, but the federal budget remains unbalanced. This fact raises a question: are the deficit-reduction benefits of the hefty OASDI asset reserves being maximized? What if Andrew Jackson's objections to interest on intragovernment transactions provided ground for amending current Social Security law? Just suppose for a moment that future legislation eliminated the interest obligation on borrowing from the OASDI trust fund. Suppose, in other words, that the interest rate that Treasury pays to borrow from OASDI became zero. It is not farfetched to imagine such a circumstance. After all, we are borrowing from ourselves and paying ourselves interest on the loans. How rational is that? It really means that the general fund of the United States is subsidizing OASDI at a time when the government is running large deficits but the trust fund is swollen with money. Should it not be the other way around?

David Pattison, an economist at the Social Security Administration, has written about this matter. He has pointed out that even "if Congress were to set the trust fund interest rate to zero, the general account would still hold funds borrowed from the trust funds rather than from the public, and the general account would still benefit from reduced cash interest payments to the public even when it no longer compensated the trust funds for the borrowed amounts." Accordingly, an "interest rate set at zero . . . would cause the regular interest payment from the general fund to the trust fund to be offset by a subsidy of equal amount from the trust fund to the general fund." Payment obligations would be transferred "to the public rather than to the trust fund." Moreover, this "trust fund subsidy to the general account" would permit reduction of the national debt, because Treasury would have to borrow less from the public. All this would facilitate "later tax decreases or expenditure increases of the same value."[29] These, of course, are worthy objectives. They would invigorate economic growth, without which debt reduction will not occur. Presumably Andrew Jackson, if

29. David Pattison, "Social Security Trust Fund Cash Flow and Reserves," *Social Security Bulletin* 75, no. 1 (2015): 14.

he had a voice today, would advocate a zero interest rate on the special-issue securities.

Yet our national affairs today are far more complex than in Jackson's era. Our population is many times greater now than then and living longer than ever; slavery has been abolished; most Americans earn their livings from pursuits other than farming; we are largely urban, and not rural; we have the largest economy in the world; consumerism rather than subsistence drives that economy; and we are now a military superpower with worldwide commitments. And, of course, we have safety-net laws that provide various kinds of insurance. This list could easily be extended. Everything is connected to other things, and they all come together in the budget, but we have not yet mastered how to prioritize and satisfy all our needs within a balanced framework. This is the fundamental reason why we confront annual deficits and run up the national debt. (Nor, it should be noted, have we tailored our tax system to meet all our needs fairly.) It is also the reason why a Jackson-style zero interest rate on OASDI special-issue securities is not an option.

Assuming that CBO and Social Security Administration projections are correct, by the 2030s the trust fund will be in difficulty. Without the interest payments, its condition would be even worse. Any perceived threat to Social Security's solvency will engender anxiety and fear among retirees and those who are approaching retirement. The consequence is certain and therefore predictable. Those dependent upon and soon-to-be-dependent upon OASDI benefits will cut back on spending. They will become increasingly marginal consumers, buying only what they consider utterly necessary. Economic growth will slow down. Layoffs will follow, and the newly unemployed will quickly cut back on their spending.

Recession will deepen. Given this scenario, the interest on the special-issue securities must be paid. The well-being of seniors, soon to be one-third of the entire population, and of the entire economy, depends upon it.

Nevertheless, we can still enjoy the short-term benefits of zero interest and the long-term benefits of a healthy OASDI fund. How? The answer, briefly put, is to *postpone the interest payments for a decade.* The year 2015 provides a useful counter-factual example. Had an interest-postponement policy been in effect that year, the budgetary deficit would have been $343 billion instead of $439 billion. (See table 2.3.) The government, in other words, would have had to borrow $96 billion less from the public than it actually did. Not only would the amount of the debt to the public have been less, but the savings would also have been realized in the interest on the debt. (Total interest on the national debt in 2015 was nearly $403 billion.)[30] More dollars would have been available to the discretionary portion of the budget, and Congress would have spent them on something—national security, education, whatever. Accordingly, the savings would have served as an additional stimulus to a still-sluggish economy. It would have promoted economic growth, which is, of course, essential to debt reduction.

Postponing interest payments to OASDI is not, however, a simple matter. Under current law, Treasury pays the interest on special-issue securities twice each year—on June 30 and December 31. But these payments exist on paper or, nowadays, on computer files. No actual transfer of cash takes place. Treasury redemption of these IOUs occurs at maturity and

---

30. TreasuryDirect, "Interest Expense on the Debt Outstanding," www.treasurydirect.gov/govt/reports/ir/ir_expense.htm. See Table I.1.

whenever, if ever, OASDI is unable to meet its obligations—namely, benefit payments and administrative costs.[31] Applying the postponed amounts to debt reduction necessarily entails real money. Where would it come from?

CBO, it will be recalled, projects that federal revenues will grow over the next decade, from 17.7 percent of GDP in 2015 to 18.3 percent in 2025. This enhancement will mainly be the product of "bracket creep" among income earners whose wages and salaries shove them into paying higher income-tax rates. It will also be a consequence of several tax features built into the Affordable Care Act (Obamacare).[32] If CBO's projection remains on course, then much, if not all, of the money needed to match what would have been pledged to OASDI will be available for deficit reduction each year over the next ten years.

Postponing interest payments to OASDI and applying the same amounts to debt reduction in future budgets will not, by themselves, eliminate altogether the gap between revenues and expenditures, but they will constitute giant steps toward that goal. Simply shrinking the deficit, as pointed out in the 2015 counterfactual example mentioned above, provides its own benefits. Note that those benefits are achievable without raising taxes or slashing programs. A temporary postponement program will get us beyond the prevailing boundaries of what to do about the annual deficits and the growing national public debt.

What needs to be done to create the kind of postponement program outlined above?

Congress needs to pass and the president needs to sign measures that

31. 2015 OASDI Trustees Report, VI, appendices, 2.
32. CBO, "The 2015 Long-Term Budget Outlook," 63–64, 66–67.

(1) unite the OASI and DI trust funds,

(2) amend existing legislation to suspend for ten years the special-issue securities that pay the interest on Treasury loans from OASDI,

(3) require the application of the sums saved by postponement to deficit reduction, and

(4) require reactivation of special-issue securities for interest on Treasury at the end of the ten-year postponement period together with the accumulated arrears as a result of the postponement. Funds to meet arrears would be derived from economic growth over the decade of postponement. If necessary, these payments might be made in installments defined by legislation.

3

A SOVEREIGN WEALTH FUND AND THE NATIONAL DEBT

T HAT WE HAVE BEEN DEBT-FREE AS A NATION FOR ONLY TWO years and ten months since 1776 has largely been forgotten. That amnesia, however, is hardly our only memory lapse. Also erased from our collective consciousness is another important fact: that during the first forty-two years under the Constitution the federal government invested taxpayer dollars in corporate securities. Alexander Hamilton, architect and engineer of our capitalist order, pioneered this approach to national development. He believed that government and the private sector should be partners in promoting economic growth. To establish that relationship and to accomplish that goal, he secured from Congress in 1791 a measure to charter a corporation—the Bank of the United States (BUS). Under Hamilton's plan, the federal government purchased 20 percent of the bank's stock for $2.0 million. The other 80 percent was sold in the open market to private investors. Hamilton hoped that profits from dividends and/or capital gains would be applied to the national debt. In 1801, however, the Jeffersonian Republicans, hostile to the bank from the beginning, came to power and divested the government of its remaining shares the following year. Nonetheless, from 1792 through 1802 the United States turned a profit in dividends and capital gains amounting to $1,153,500, or 57.6 percent of the original investment, and almost five percent of principal payments on the national debt during that same period.[1] What was the return on the investment compared to GDP over that same period?

Accordingly, the average GDP over the eleven-year period amounted to approximately $ 0.4418181 billion, or $441.818 million. (See table 3.1) Therefore, the government's bank profit of $1,153,500 for the same period represented about 25 percent of GDP.

In 1811, the Jeffersonians did not recharter the bank. Crisis ensued because the following year Congress declared war on England but was financially unprepared to wage it. The one institution with the capacity to extend credit to the government no longer existed, but in the end the United States survived both militarily and financially. It had not been easy, and the experience chastened many within Jeffersonian ranks. Leaders like Henry Clay and John C. Calhoun, even President Madison, who had opposed the bank in 1791, began to reconsider the bank question. In 1816 Congress chartered a second Bank of the United States, and again the government purchased 20 percent of the outstanding stock. Indeed, it

1. Carl Lane, "For 'A Positive Profit': The Federal Investment in the First Bank of the United States, 1792–1802," *William and Mary Quarterly* 54 (July 1997): 601–12.

Table 3.1
Estimated United States GDP, 1792–1802
(In Billions)

1792	0.270
1793	0.300
1794	0.350
1795	0.420
1796	0.470
1797	0.450
1798	0.460
1799	0.500
1800	0.520
1801	0.580
1802	0.540

(Source: Louis Johnston and Samuel H. Williamson, "What Was the US GDP then?," *MeasuringWorth*, 2015.)

went beyond the bank investment and purchased stock in a number of canal companies.[2] This is of extraordinary importance. Why? Because this approach to national development did not trouble lawmakers. It simply constituted revitalization and extension of Hamilton's vision of government and private-sector partnership. In 1825, the Committee on Roads and Canals reported to the House of Representatives: "The committee cannot conceive how the General Government can aid in the internal improvements of the country . . . with greater propriety than by subscriptions to [the stock of] com-

2. Carl Lane, "Federal Investments in Private Canal Companies, 1825–1835," unpublished paper presented at the Annual Conference of the Economic and Business Historical Society, Albany, NY, April 26, 2001. Copy on file at the Felician University library.

panies incorporated by the respective states."[3] Even Andrew Jackson, in his post–War of 1812 career as senator from Tennessee, supported these investments.

The canal investments, however, unlike the investment in the second BUS, lost money. While the bank paid the government about $500,000 a year in dividends, the canal investments wound up losing about $800,000 *in toto*. Losses, however, did not deter the companies from repeatedly petitioning the government for additional stock subsidies to avoid bankruptcy.

Matters changed when Jackson became president. By then national debt freedom was only four years away, and Jackson apparently changed his mind about the propriety of government investment in corporate stock. Such investment, then as today, entailed risk. Jackson evidently believed that the risk was worth the potential benefit as long as debt freedom remained on the distant financial horizon. But the nearer debt freedom drew, the less acceptable the risk of losses became. In May 1830, he broke the post–War of 1812, neo-Hamiltonian partnership between government and the private sector. He vetoed a bill for government purchase of stock in a company building a highway from Maysville to Lexington in Kentucky. It is true that he had several reasons for the veto, but one was that a company failure could result in new taxes or new government debt, or both.[4] Neither was acceptable. In his State of the Union message to Congress later that year, Jackson elaborated on his opposition to government involvement in the private sector. It put public money under the control of corporate executives who were

3. Lane, *A Nation Wholly Free*, 163.
4. James D. Richardson, ed., *A Compilation of the Messages and Papers of the Presidents, 1789–1897*, 10 vols. (Washington, DC, 1896–99), II, 1046–56.

not accountable to government. It exposed government officials to the charge of "favoritism." After all, why should one
company be subsidized but not another? Finally, those enterprises that enjoyed federal subsidy kept coming back for more
when they incurred losses. "The bill authorizing a subscrip-
tion to the Louisville and Portland Canal affords a striking
illustration of the difficulty of withholding additional appropriations," Jackson wrote, "when the first erroneous step has
been taken by instituting a partnership between the
Government and private companies. It proposes a third sub-
scription on the part of the United States, when each preced-
ing one was . . . regarded as the extent of the aid" that the
government would provide.[5]

Ever since Jackson's 1830 policy statement, the United
States, except for less than a handful of emergency circum-
stances, has not purchased corporate stocks and bonds.
Jackson terminated the Hamiltonian government–private
sector marriage in national development. The divorce decree
Jackson handed down endures to this day.

Yet times have changed. National debt freedom is not on
a short financial horizon. Indeed, it is not on any horizon at
all. Some say debt freedom is unachievable. But if we espouse
the views of Andrew Jackson in the early 1820s and not the
early 1830s, we might avail ourselves of revenue benefits that
do not entail tax increases—revenues that can be applied to
narrowing the annual budgetary deficits and reducing the
need to borrow. It is time to resurrect the Hamiltonian
approach and begin investing in the securities markets.

How would such an undertaking be accomplished? The
short answer to that question is this: with extraordinary diffi-

5. Ibid., II, 1073.

culty. Why? Because there is a large and powerful segment of our society that would denounce such an effort as "socialism," a dirty word in our political and cultural lexicon. Neither Alexander Hamilton nor Andrew Jackson was, of course, a socialist. Indeed, the idea of socialism was just emerging in the early nineteenth century in forms we commonly call "utopian," and was being experimented with in Europe and in the United States. Brook Farm in Massachusetts is probably the most famous example of the latter. None succeeded, but there was no negative visceral reaction to the concept. In fact, Robert Owen, the Scottish socialist and founder of the New Harmony community in Indiana, was invited to address Congress in 1824. His views were not attacked as un-American, and he was warmly welcomed. American fear of socialism is a twentieth-century phenomenon. It had nothing to do with Jackson's termination of the government–private sector partnership. Nonetheless, recreating that relationship will unleash a firestorm of anti-socialist attack, and countering it will not be easy.

The Hamiltonian approach is not socialist at all. Rather, it is an affirmation of capitalism. The private-for-profit enterprise system has served the American people well, at least most of the time. It creates jobs, pays good salaries and wages, generates consumer products that make life easier, offers possible homeownership to many, as well as numerous other investment opportunities. It is the mother of the American Dream. It needs to be remembered, however, that the benefits of capitalism come to us as individuals, not to all of us as a single community composed of "We the People," at least not since Andrew Jackson's day. All Americans benefitted collectively from the federal investment in the second Bank of the

United States. The annual half-million-dollar dividend the bank paid to the Treasury was a half million less than what taxpayers would have had to reach into their pockets and come up with. In other words, the United States' bank stock served as tax relief for everyone. It was a painless means to raise revenue.

Many governments around the world have adopted the Hamiltonian approach to public-private partnership. They have created government-owned corporations and appropriated money to them. Boards of directors (or trustees) oversee and manage, usually through committees, investments in stocks and bonds, whether corporate or public, in order to generate profits. Ordinarily, the principal amount is not expended but only the earnings—interest, dividends, capital gains—on whatever the host government's investment purpose is: to underwrite education, transportation, hospitals, the arts, whatever. In this sense, they resemble college or university endowments. These governmental efforts are commonly called sovereign wealth funds. They are hardly socialist, because their success depends upon a healthy capitalist order, and they themselves seek profits.[6]

It is exceedingly important to know (and surprising given the potential socialist branding) that many of our states, including red ones, have sovereign wealth funds. Gar Alperovitz and Thomas M. Hanna called our attention to these funds in a *New York Times* op-ed piece in 2015. They pointed out, among other matters, that nowadays many conservatives are willing to accept these governmental intrusions

6. For an overview of sovereign wealth funds, see Shai Bernstein, Josh Lerner, and Antoinette Schoar, "The Investment Strategies of Sovereign Wealth Funds," *Journal of Economic Perspectives* 27, no. 2 (Spring 2013): 219–38.

into the economy in order to get corresponding tax relief. They observed that "the most well-known case is Alaska."[7] In fact, the Alaska Permanent Fund, as it is called, is not only the most famous; it is also the most well-endowed. On July 13, 2015, its total assets amounted to an astounding $54,313,700,000. Its holdings were well diversified: US and non-US stocks and bonds, real estate, cash reserve, and more. Royalties from mineral mining, especially from oil extraction, feed the fund. Every year Alaska residents receive a dividend check.[8] The recent downturn in oil prices has interrupted this policy and process, but for how long remains to be seen.

Alaska's sovereign wealth fund is not unique. Texas, in fact, has two of them. The Texas Permanent School Fund dates all the way back to 1854. Today, it secures its funds from royalties on oil, natural gas, and other mineral resources. With a balance of $37.7 billion, it is now the largest educational fund in the United States.[9] Its earnings help to underwrite K–12 education throughout the state. Texas's other sovereign wealth fund is its University Fund. Like the Permanent Fund, it earns income from royalties on natural resources and essentially serves as an endowment to the University of Texas system. With $25.4 billion in assets, it recently displaced Yale as the second-largest university endowment in the United States.[10]

Oregon provides another example. Its Common School Fund derives revenue from leased rangelands, timber-producing forests, and other natural resources. Managed by the State Land Board, in 2009 the fund distributed $40 million to the

7. Gar Alperovitz and Thomas M. Hanna, "Socialism, American-Style," *The New York Times*, July 23, 2015, A27.
8. Alaska Permanent Fund Corporation, www.apfc.org.
9. For more information, google "Texas Permanent School Fund."
10. For more information, google "Texas University Fund."

state's 197 school districts. At the end of June 2013, the fund's assets amounted to $1.20 billion, and a year later totaled $1.45 billion.[11] These values may not compare well with Alaska's or Texas's, but they are not small amounts of money either.

Wyoming's Permanent Mineral Trust Fund constitutes another example. Established in 1974 by amendment to the state's constitution, it earns revenue from a 1.5 percent severance tax on the gross value of mineral products extracted within Wyoming. This tax grows the fund's principal, which, by law, cannot be expended. Only earnings on principal are applied to state purposes. Today the fund's balance stands at $5.6 billion, a hefty sum.[12]

Louisiana also has a sovereign wealth fund. Its Education Quality Trust Fund was established in 1986 as a result of a settlement with the federal government over mineral rights. The state was awarded $541 million, which became the seed money for the fund dedicated to educational "enrichment." The fund's value today is $1.3 billion.[13]

Louisiana and Texas are not the only deep southern states with sovereign wealth funds. The Alabama Trust Fund belongs on that list. It was established in 1985 and secures its revenue from royalties on oil and gas produced in the state. Most earnings on principal are allocated to the state's criminal justice system. At the outset, the fund was worth $334 million. Its value today is unclear.[14]

Other states with sovereign wealth funds are New Mexico, North Dakota, and West Virginia. New Mexico's State

11. Google "Oregon Common School Fund." Multiple links.

12. For more information, google "Permanent Wyoming Mineral Trust Fund."

13. For more information, google "Louisiana Education Quality Trust Fund."

14. For more information, google "Alabama Trust Fund."

Investment Council was created in 1958, and, like several other sovereign funds, draws revenue from oil and gas production. The fund aims at preserving principal and contributing earnings to the state's operating budget. Today the fund's balance amounts to $19.8 billion.[15]

North Dakota's Legacy Fund was created by legislation in 2009 and became operative in 2011. It, too, depends on revenue from oil and natural gas. Indeed, 30 percent of all taxes derived from those commodities are now deposited into the Legacy Fund. In 2017 earnings will be transferred to the state treasury, and the legislature will determine how to expend them.[16]

West Virginia offers a final example. In 2014, its legislature created the West Virginia Future Fund. It also depends upon revenues earned from mineral extraction: coal, natural gas, and other natural resources—specifically, 25 percent of all severance taxes on mineral commodities in excess of $175,000. The money is transferred to the state treasury and administered by the West Virginia Investment Management Board. Investment income will not be spent before 2020, but thereafter the interest and other income generated by the Future Fund will be applied to state education, infrastructure, and other needs.[17]

If these state sovereign wealth funds constitute socialism, then socialism is alive and well in the United States today. But, of course, they are not socialist but capitalist through and through. The blue and red states that have them are benefitting in many ways: funding education, infrastructure, criminal

15. For more information, google "New Mexico State Investment Council."
16. For more information, google "North Dakota Legacy Fund."
17. For more information, google "West Virginia Future Fund."

justice, and closing state budget deficits. They are pointing to the direction the entire nation should follow. Many nations have sovereign wealth funds. Some of them, like several of our states, seed their investment enterprises with monies generated from oil or other commodities. Norway is a case in point. Its sovereign wealth fund, seeded by oil revenues, is worth $882 billion.[18] The United Arab Emirates also have a very large fund. Its Abu Dhabi Investment Authority's assets total $773 billion.[19] Saudi Arabia also has a substantial investment enterprise, Sama Foreign Holdings. Its investment assets amount to $671.8 billion.[20] Kuwait is not too far behind. The Kuwait Investment Authority holds $592 billion.[21] Qatar, another oil exporting country, also enjoys a sovereign wealth fund worth $256 billion.[22] Typically, or standard with sovereign wealth practice, investments are made in foreign corporate or governmental securities. (This is one of the reasons why so much of the American public debt is held by foreign entities.)

Not all sovereign wealth funds are rooted in profits from oil or other natural resources. Some are seeded by profits from exporting manufactured goods. China is one such example. It has at least two sovereign wealth funds. The SAFE Investment Company, for instance, holds assets to the tune of $567.9 billion while the Chinese Investment Corporation is worth $746.7 billion.[23] Before the recent economic crisis in China, their combined value amounted to $1.314.600 trillion, an

18. Google "Sovereign Wealth Fund Institute Rankings."
19. Ibid.
20. Ibid.
21. Ibid.
22. Ibid.
23. Ibid.

enormous sum. Their current value is unclear. Another example of an export-based fund is one of Singapore's. GIC Private Limited is worth $344 billion.[24]

Other nations with sovereign wealth funds include Russia, Kazakhstan, Libya, Iran, Algeria, Brunei, Nigeria, and Azerbaijan. Others, such as Israel, are preparing to emulate them. Why? Because they generate revenue for public purposes in a painless way. Alexander Hamilton, in the early days of our republic, knew and understood this. His method of achieving revenue enhancement through investment in the private sector was, of course, different from what we call sovereign wealth funds. He envisioned individual acts of Congress as the means of investing in corporate stocks. Yet, methodology aside, today the United States has no sovereign wealth fund.

Creating an American SWF will require, at the very least, an act of Congress chartering such a corporation and appropriating to it the seed money (principal) which will be invested. The law will also need to establish the management structure that will govern the overall investment process and set up accountability mechanisms. The latter must entail safeguards against insider trading, because the injection of large amounts of American taxpayer dollars into the worldwide market will likely cause stock prices to rise generally, but most sharply in the shares of those firms the SWF purchased.

At least two good reasons warrant the creation of an American sovereign wealth fund. First, despite the fact that the government's public debt is large ($13.8 trillion), its GDP is larger. Ours is the largest economy in the world, and we generate new wealth all the time. An SWF provides a means of capturing a portion of that wealth and perpetuating it as

24. Google "Sovereign Wealth Fund Institute Rankings."

long as principal remains untouchable. Second, an SWF, generating a return on its investments, raises revenue without new or increased taxes. Accordingly, it will enhance the capacity of the government to close the gap between income and expenditure and hasten the arrival of a balanced budget. Balancing the budget, it will be recalled, will mean shrinking the interest payments due on the public debt, widening the discretionary portion of the budget, and promoting more vigorous economic growth. (The Dow, Standard and Poors, and Nasdaq will likely see their indices rise.) Prosperity is enhanced, and over time the size of the public debt grows smaller.

Most sovereign wealth funds around the world, with some exceptions, annually earn about 6 percent on their investments. Imagine Congress creating an SWF and appropriating to it $100 billion, profits to be applied to deficit reduction. Imagine also, to be conservative in our expectations, that this government-owned corporation earned only 5 percent each year on its investments. Such a result would apply five billion to the operating budget each year, or fifty billion over a decade. After ten years, income from the SWF together with the postponed interest payments to OASI and DI, will, hopefully, have virtually eliminated the gap between revenue and expenditure and permit beginning the repayment of interest and the arrears of interest to the Social Security trust fund. This matter, it will be recalled, is of vital importance to assure that senior citizens remain robust consumers within the American economy. The most important word in the sentence before the last is, of course, "hopefully." The future is always unpredictable. Fortunately, the era of Andrew Jackson has more guidance to offer with respect to addressing our public debt problem.

4

OVERSEAS DEPLOYMENTS AND THE NATIONAL DEBT

S INTEREST ON OUR PUBLIC DEBT INCREASES, THE MONEY available for discretionary spending shrinks. At the same time, mandatory spending for Social Security, Medicare, Medicaid, and the subsidies embedded in Obamacare will increase over time. Less and less will become available for education, infrastructure, and other necessities, including defense. Yet the defense budget is likely to remain the largest appropriation on the discretionary menu.

Few Americans would dispute the need for more than a merely adequate defense posture. We live in dangerous times, as the recent terrorist attacks in Paris, San Bernardino, Brussels, and Orlando have demonstrated. Indeed, to universal disappointment, the end of the Cold War did not usher in an era of peace; nor did it deliver the much touted "peace dividend"—savings on defense spending that would have bene-

fitted American taxpayers. Instead, a decade after the evapo-
ration of the Soviet Union in 1991, the United States suffered
the 9/11 massacres. Many Americans who had never heard of
Al Qaeda before suddenly learned we were at war with a
stateless terrorist organization capable of delivering death and
destruction on American territory. The war against terror had
begun. We attacked Afghanistan and overturned the Taliban
regime there. Two years later, we attacked Iraq and eliminated
Saddam Hussein's government. These efforts ballooned our
national debt and are in large measure the causes of our current debt problem. Accordingly, it is incumbent upon us to
review very carefully how we spend each and every defense
dollar.

Military expenditures are, of course, always under review.
Can contracts with vendors be renegotiated at less cost? Can
equipment be purchased more cheaply from other suppliers?
The various armed services are always looking, as they
should, for cost savings, but do budget reviews entail reexamination of the rationale for the expenditure in the first place?
Put another way, does the original purpose for the expenditure remain pertinent to today's realities? These questions
merit investigation, especially for "big-item" expenses like
military bases overseas. Are some simply relics of bygone eras?
Have any outlived their original *raison d'etre*? Which continue
to receive funding as a result of bureaucratic inertia? If the
budgetary justification for any of them has undergone repeat-
ed change, does that mean no valid purpose warrants their
perpetuation? The history of each of our overseas bases can
serve to answer these questions and, very possibly, reduce our
annual budgetary deficit. History, in short, can serve to
enlighten both our foreign and defense policies to secure
financial benefits.

The Jacksonian era has important guidance to offer with regard to American foreign and defense policy as those matters bear on national indebtedness. Despite his reputation for belligerence and violence, Andrew Jackson and his administrations were not particularly assertive on the international stage—at least not until the national debt was extinguished and surpluses began to flood the United States Treasury with millions of dollars. Then, and only then, did Jackson feel financially equipped to risk as well as to wage war to secure what the United States was entitled to under international law and custom. The French crisis of 1835 exemplifies this point.

Jackson informed Congress of problems with France in his 1834 State of the Union report, the same message in which he announced national debt freedom. The difficulty had been brewing for several years. In 1831 the American minister to France, William C. Rives, had negotiated a treaty with France on a matter that had chilled relations between both countries for some time: compensation for American commercial losses during the Napoleonic conflicts. The government of King Louis Philippe agreed to pay 25 million francs in half a dozen installments. Payments were to begin a year after both countries ratified the agreement.[1]

Both countries did ratify, and the documents were formally exchanged on February 2, 1832. Accordingly, the initial payment was due on February 1, 1833. The French Chamber of Deputies, however, did not appropriate the money, and in 1834 it simply refused to pay. In July that same year, another legislature also refused to pay.[2]

1. Lane, *A Nation Wholly Free*, 176.
2. Ibid., 176.

Jackson was outraged and would not acquiesce in France's refusal to honor the treaty. He rejected any further negotiation. He demanded the agreement's prompt implementation; otherwise he would take unilateral action. International law, he maintained, provided nations victimized in the way France was victimizing the United States with an appropriate "remedy." The United States had the right to seize property belonging to France or its citizens, and Jackson asked Congress for legislation "authorizing reprisals" against French property. Congress, however, took no action. Yet Jackson's bellicose posture regarding French non-compliance with the treaty meant that the United States might be sliding into armed conflict with France. America's new financial condition—debt freedom—had conjoined with national security. Jackson's supporters in Congress pushed to get the budding surplus spent on defense. Yet Congress, because of intense partisanship, could not get its act together, and failed to pass any defense measure.[3]

In his next annual message to Congress, December 1835, Jackson reported that the French Chamber of Deputies had considered his recommendation for reprisals the year before as an insult to France's national honor and had broken diplomatic relations with the United States. Informal but promising discussions continued nonetheless, and for a time it seemed that the impasse would be resolved. But as an appropriation bill made its way through the Chamber of Deputies, an amendment provided that no money should be paid until the French government received "satisfactory explanations" for Jackson's 1834 remarks regarding retaliation. For the president, this constituted a demand for an apology. Jackson, of

3. Lane, *A Nation Wholly Free*, 176.

course, told Congress that he would never apologize. The United States and France seemed headed to war against each other. While the United States was not militarily prepared for armed conflict, financially it was; Treasury would not need to borrow. Debt freedom meant its coffers were spilling over. In the end, however, the surplus was not needed to wage war. Great Britain's timely intervention in the Franco-American crisis preserved the peace.[4]

Times, of course, have changed. Today we are an unmatched global military superpower, but concurrently we are saddled with a public debt whose interest obligations are eroding our capabilities. The CBO's 2015 report explained that after the Cold War defense spending fell to 2.9 percent of GDP in 2000. Then came 9/11. Subsequently, "military operations in Iraq and Afghanistan" forced spending upward to an average of 4.6 percent of GDP between 2009 and 2011. It fell, however, to 3.5 percent of GDP in 2014, a reduction resulting from the cutback in military operations in Iraq and Afghanistan and the Budget Control Act of 2011, otherwise known as the sequester.[5] Nevertheless, defense spending remains by far the largest element of the annual discretionary budget. The Department of Defense's budgetary request for fiscal year 2015 exceeded $495 billion, more than half the entire discretionary portion of the budget.[6] It is the obvious place to look for ways and means to shrink the annual budgetary shortfalls.

---

4. Ibid., 178. For a full account of the French crisis, see John M. Belohlavek, *"Let the Eagle Soar!"*: *The Foreign Policy of Andrew Jackson* (Lincoln: University of Nebraska Press, 1985), chapter 4.

5. CBO, "The 2015 Long-Term Budget Outlook," 57–58.

6. United States Department of Defense Fiscal Year 2015 (March 2014), 117. See also: www.nationalpriorities.org/campaigns/military-spending-united-states/.

Can history serve as a guide on this matter? To answer that question, it may be useful to consider the circumstances that flipped our financial and military circumstances from those that existed in the Age of Jackson to those that prevail today.

Defeating fascism in Europe and the Japanese in Asia transformed the United States into a superpower for the first time in its history. Indeed, when World War II ended in 1945, US military power was unchallengeable. It had, until 1949, a monopoly on atomic weaponry. The world had changed. Great Britain was no longer the predominant force in the West. In early 1947, it acknowledged its new status in the world by informing the Truman administration that it could no longer, as it had for decades, police the eastern Mediterranean and help Greece and Turkey suppress insurgencies that were allegedly communist in character. The message was clear. Only the United States could take Britain's place in that part of the world, and President Truman accepted the challenge and the responsibility. The result was the Truman Doctrine, a March 1947 American pledge "to support free peoples who are resisting attempted subjugation by armed minorities."[7] The president sought and secured from Congress $400 million in aid to Greece and Turkey, which turned out to be a down payment on an emerging struggle with the Soviet Union. The cost rose sharply a few months later. The European Recovery Program, commonly called the Marshall Plan, injected $12.4 billion into Western Europe to thwart communist ambitions there. Ambiguity vanished. The United States and its former ally against Nazi Germany, the Soviet Union, were now engaged in a Cold War—one that threatened to turn hot on many subsequent occasions.

7. Quoted in William H. Chafe, *The Unfinished Journey: America Since World War II*, 6th ed. (New York: Oxford University Press, 2007), 63.

One of the more peace-endangering Cold War episodes began in 1948. The Soviet Union attempted to deny the Western powers access to West Berlin by blockading the city. President Truman responded to the challenge by airlifting supplies to Berlin, and, after many months, the Soviet dictator, Josef Stalin, ended the blockade. The Berlin crisis had far-reaching ramifications. In 1949 the United States led the way to creating the North Atlantic Treaty, which embodied the American strategy of containment: not allowing Soviet communism to expand into Western Europe. The treaty's principal provision, Article V, was that an attack on one member state would be counted as an attack on all. Twelve nations joined the treaty organization (NATO): Belgium, Canada, Denmark, France, Iceland, Italy, Luxembourg, the Netherlands, Norway, Portugal, the United Kingdom, and, of course, the United States. The creation of multiple military bases throughout much of Western Europe resulted, with the United States picking up much of the staffing and the tab.

The Soviet Union responded to NATO by emulating it. It established a counter-alliance with its satellite states in Eastern Europe: the Warsaw Pact. By 1950 Europe was divided into armed and hostile camps. Each menaced the other, but the peace did not break, even though NATO grew. In 1952, Greece and Turkey signed on as members, and in 1955 West Germany did the same. Spain followed their example in 1982.

Years of recurring crises—most notably the 1962 Cuban Missile crisis—ensued, but the Cold War, conflicts in Korea and Vietnam notwithstanding, never turned hot. Ultimately, it ended without so much as a puff of smoke. In December 1991, the Soviet Parliament, for reasons that need not be discussed here, voted to dissolve the regime. NATO's *raison d'etre* vanished. So, too, did the Warsaw Pact. Yet, remarkably, NATO did not.

Indeed, not only has NATO endured into the post–Cold War era, but its numbers have grown. It has increased its membership eastward, enrolling in its ranks former members of the Soviet bloc. In 1997, for example, Hungary, Poland, and the Czech Republic enlisted in NATO. In 2004 Bulgaria, Estonia, Latvia, Lithuania, Romania, and Slovakia did the same. Most recently, in 2009, Albania and Croatia joined. As a result, today twenty-seven states comprise NATO. Yet NATO's *raison d'etre*, the Soviet Union, no longer exists.

What is NATO's purpose in the twenty-first century? This is a question that may keep Vladimir Putin awake at night. He is surely aware that over the last few centuries Western powers have attacked Russia several times: Sweden in the eighteenth century, Napoleonic France in the nineteenth, and Germany twice in the twentieth. Remembering these elements of Russian history in the midst of post–Cold War NATO expansion might well induce anxiety, even paranoia. It at least makes understandable, to some degree, Putin's "acting out" in Georgia in 2008 and the Ukraine in 2014–15. (Neither Georgia nor Ukraine is a NATO member, so therefore Putin has not directly challenged the alliance, but he clearly wants to be certain that neither country signs on to the treaty.) In any event, it is probably too late to undo whatever damages the perpetuation of NATO has done to American–Russian relations. It is not too late, however, to undo the financial burden that NATO imposes on the United States.

Preserving and extending NATO, a Cold War relic, has cost and continues to cost the United States vast amounts of money. Given our annual budgetary imbalances, this is a matter that merits serious review. Let's look at the number of US troops stationed in NATO countries in FY 2015.

Table 4.1
US Troops Stationed in NATO Countries, FY 2015

Country	Current Number of US Troops[8]
ORIGINAL MEMBERS	
Belgium	1,174
Canada	147
Denmark	20
France	71
Iceland	0
Italy	10,922
Luxembourg	6
Netherlands	374
Norway	88
Portugal	743
United Kingdom	9,846
United States	0
1952 ADDITIONS	
Greece	351
Turkey	1,505
1955 ADDITION	
Germany	47,761
1982 ADDITION	
Spain	1,727
1997 ADDITIONS	
Czech Republic	13

8. "How Many US Troops Are Overseas?," www.vetfriends.com/us-deployments-overseas/index.cfm.

Hungary	63
Poland	37
2004 ADDITIONS	
Bulgaria	15
Estonia	10
Latvia	5
Lithuania	8
Romania	37
Slovakia	10
2009 ADDITIONS	
Albania	7
Croatia	11
TOTAL	74,951

These numbers tell us a lot, even though not all American forces in NATO member states are under NATO control. Others are under the US European Command and operate under arrangements between the United States and the host government. This distinction, however, makes little difference. The costs of these deployments to American taxpayers are significant.[9]

At first glance, it is clear that the number of American troops in each of the post-Cold War NATO member states is not large. Hungary, with just over sixty, represents the biggest contingent. Collectively, they total 216, less than one percent of all our forces in NATO countries. They do not threaten Russia or any other country—at least not yet. But, as David Vine of American University has written—and no one has

9. The United States, largest contributor to NATO because it has the largest economy, provides approximately 22 percent of NATO's civil, military, and Security Investment Programme (NSIP) budgets. See 2016 executive summaries of these budgets at NATO's website.

studied our overseas installations more thoroughly than Professor Vine—military bases, like other organizations, acquire lives of their own through "bureaucratic inertia" and, once established, tend to get bigger.[10]

Indeed, shutting down bases provides no guarantee that they will not come back to life. Iceland, one of the original twelve NATO members, serves as an example. The United States closed the Keflavik Naval Air Station in 2006. In the fall of 2015, however, American deputy secretary of defense Robert Work traveled to Reykjavik to discuss reopening the base with government officials there. The justification concerns Russian air and submarine activity in Iceland's vicinity.[11] How large the American redeployment will be remains to be seen. Yet one wonders what Russia's aim or aims might be. It is difficult to believe that Russia contemplates an assault on Icelandic sovereignty. After all, what would it gain other than a huge military conflict with the alliance?

The vast bulk of American troops are stationed in NATO member states that predate the end of the Cold War. They total 74,735, more than 99 percent of American military personnel on duty in the allied countries. Germany currently hosts the largest number, almost forty-eight thousand, or approximately 64 percent of the total. They are spread out over 174 bases in that country.[12] Moreover, the larger installations—the "Little Americas," as Professor Vine calls them—

10. David Vine, *Base Nation: How US Military Bases Abroad Harm America and the World* (New York: Metropolitan Books, 2015), 332. Vine does not focus only on the financial burdens of our overseas bases but also on how they damage the environment, encourage anti-Americanism, promote host-country crime, and other problems.
11. Trude Petterson, "US Military Returns to Iceland," *Independent Barents Observer*, February 10, 2016.
12. Vine, *Base Nation*, 3.

house the families of military personnel. Family residence on bases has been standard policy for many years. Supporting wives, husbands, and children on these bases ups the cost to the American taxpayer. These Little Americas attempt to create suburban, middle-class American communities. They provide schools, restaurants, movie theaters, athletic facilities, country clubs, and all the elements of stereotypical life in the United States. Construction and maintenance, of course, elevate the costs.[13]

The second-largest US troop deployment to a country whose NATO membership predated the end of the Cold War is to Italy. It hosts nearly eleven thousand American servicemen at fifty bases, nearly 15 percent of the total US military personnel presently serving in NATO member states.[14] As in Germany, the larger bases constitute Little Americas, and serve as residences not only to the servicemen and women but to their families as well. Also, as in Germany, the American middle-class lifestyle these communities provide, together with construction and maintenance, drives up the cost of our presence.

NATO is not the only relic of an earlier era contributing to our annual budgetary deficits and burdening American taxpayers with extraordinary expenses. Our deployments in Asia do the same things. Japan is a prime example. By Professor Vine's count, the United States currently maintains 113 military installations in that country. (If the islands of Japan were united into one landmass, the result would approximate the size of California.) More than fifty thousand American military personnel serve there.[15] More than fifteen

13. Ibid., 48–52 and passim.
14. Ibid., 122, 235.

thousand Marines are on duty in Okinawa alone, at a cost of between $150 and $225 million more than if they were stationed in the United States.[16] The total annual cost of our presence in Japan is about a "billion dollars a year."[17]

Why this huge expensive presence? At the end of the Pacific War in 1945, the United States occupied Japan. Under General Douglas MacArthur's leadership, Japan's society and government both underwent numerous changes. Among the most important was the adoption of a new constitution establishing a democratic parliamentary system and, in Article IX, banning war as a legitimate instrument of foreign policy. (Japan did, of course, create a self-defense force because, under the United Nations Charter, all nations enjoy the right to defend themselves. Nowadays Japan's defense force is quite large.) When the Korean War began in 1950, Japan became a major supplier of resources for the troops who went to the peninsula to drive back the communist North Koreans and, when China joined the conflict, to support the American-led United Nations forces against them as well. Japan's economy, which had been devastated in the war against the United States, began to revive rapidly. When a peace treaty was finally struck between Japan and the United States in 1952, a mutual defense treaty accompanied it. Under its provisions, Japan granted the United States the right to maintain military bases on its territory to protect against communist aggression by China and/or North Korea, or even, perhaps, the Soviet Union. The Cold War justified the American military presence in Japan, and from time to time the defense treaty has been renewed, much to the chagrin of many Japanese.

15. Ibid., 3, 275.
16. Ibid., 275.
17. Ibid., 275.

Yet sixty-four years have passed since the first treaty. In the interim, neither North Korea, China, nor the Soviet Union before its demise in 1991 ever attacked Japan. Moreover, even though several factors have caused tensions between Japan and its Asian neighbors, it seems exceedingly unlikely that China or North Korea will attack Japan. Some will say that the mutual defense treaty and its resulting American military presence constituted a deterrent. Perhaps, but if China or North Korea launched an attack against Japan today, would ground troops crossing the Sea of Japan on ships invade the islands, or would manned aircraft, missiles, or both character-ize the attack? The answer is obvious, and the same pattern would, of course, characterize the Japanese and American counterattack. Would all fifty thousand of our military on duty in Japan have roles to play? What would the fifteen thousand Marines at Okinawa do? In short, do we really need that much personnel stationed there? A reexamination of the reasons for each of the 113 installations in Japan is in order, because the deployments are expensive. Eliminating redun-dancies, bureaucratic inertia, and bases whose *raison d'etre* keeps changing can result in significant savings. Given our budgetary deficits, such reexaminations will serve our nation-al interest.

Much is the same concerning our presence in South Korea. After the 1953 armistice ending the war there, the Eisenhower administration established—and its successors maintained—American troop deployments south of the Demilitarized Zone (DMZ) to protect South Korea from another attack. Approximately thirty thousand American troops manned bases there, especially along the DMZ. At that time, the regime in South Korea had not yet recovered from the impact of WWII, not to mention the more recent conflict in which it was overrun first by the North Koreans and then the Chinese. It had no capacity to defend itself against another onslaught. Accordingly, the US presence made sense, not because thirty thousand Americans could defeat the million-plus-man army at the North's disposal, but because the government in Pyongyang would know that wiping out so many Americans would result in a devastating air attack, including, very possibly, a nuclear strike. The thirty thousand, although severely outnumbered, in effect kept the peace on the peninsula.

More than sixty years have passed since the Korean armistice, and much has changed. The Cold War context of the 1950–1953 conflict no longer exists. South Korea has built a thriving economy and maintains a modern, well-equipped, and well-trained military. In fact, every year the United States and South Korea engage in joint military exercises, much to the chagrin of the government in the North, which expresses its displeasure by planting mines in the DMZ, firing short- and medium-range missiles into the sea, and conducting nuclear tests. These actions, especially the latter, are as provocative as the regime's belligerent rhetoric, yet peace on the peninsula has not collapsed. Why not? Probably because Kim Jong-un and his inner circle know what the consequence of breaking the peace will be. Indeed, as "crazy" as those in power in Pyongyang may seem to be, they are not stupid. They surely remember that after 9/11, when three thousand Americans died, we promptly overthrew Afghanistan's Taliban government, and two years later toppled Saddam Hussein from power in Iraq. In other words, unless the regime in North Korea is suicidal, which it is not, then peace on the peninsula will endure. The communist dynasty in North Korea has one principal goal: to survive and to perpetuate its power into the future. In the process it will learn what China, India, and Pakistan have learned—that acquiring nuclear weapons does not mean that they can be used. It means, in fact, the very opposite. Any nation that employs a nuclear weapon against another nation engages in self-termination. Using a nuclear weapon guarantees a nuclear counterattack. Possession of nuclear weapons merely provides a certain prestige, the reputation for and the appearance of power, but not the substance of power itself.

If these conjectures are correct, then the question arises: why do we have eighty-three military bases in South Korea today?[18] Osan Base and Camps Humphreys, Casey, Kim, and Stanley are among the largest. Altogether, today the total US troop presence in South Korea amounts to approximately 29,500. South Korea is not a large country. It is difficult to believe that our presence there is free of redundancies. Identifying and eliminating them may save millions and millions of dollars.

All of this brings us to the oldest relic in the history of American military deployments overseas—the naval base at Guantanamo Bay, Cuba. The United States secured possession of the area, approximately forty-five square miles, as one consequence of the 1898 Spanish-American War. Cuba, a Spanish colony for centuries, had been struggling for independence for decades, and over time the colonial authorities countered with increasingly oppressive methods. By the mid-1890s their techniques outraged much of American public opinion. Pressure on President William McKinley to intervene on behalf of the rebels became irresistible after the USS *Maine* blew up in Cuban waters. The United States declared war

18. Vine, *Base Nation*, 3.

against Spain, and the Teller amendment to the war authorization said quite bluntly that, at the conclusion of hostilities, the United States would recognize Cuba as a self-governing sovereign nation state.[19] That pledge, however, did not last long. Three years later Senator Orville Platt of Connecticut sponsored an amendment to an army appropriations bill requiring, among other things, that the Cuban constitution then being drafted in Havana grant the United States the right to intercede militarily on the island whenever it wished, and to provide it territory for naval bases.[20] The Platt amendment effectively canceled the Teller amendment, and the new Cuban government wound up accepting, under duress, less than full independence. (What truly independent nation allows another nation to intervene militarily in its affairs?) American military personnel had occupied Guantanamo from the earliest days of the war. Now they were there for good.

Why? What was the aim of the American post–Spanish-American War presence at Guantanamo? As Professor Jonathan M. Hansen at Harvard University has pointed out in his superb study, *Guantanamo: An American History*, for the next few decades following implementation of the Platt amendment, the Guantanamo base served to maintain order on the island. American investment there had increased from $80 million in 1901 to $220 million in 1911, and exceeded a billion by 1923.[21] The Guantanamo base's mission was to protect these investments, and it did. Because of disorders, beginning in 1906 the American military occupied the entire

19. Jonathan M. Hansen, *Guantanamo: An American History* (New York: Hill and Wang, 2011), 88.
20. Ibid., 134.
21. Ibid., 150.

island for three years.[22] Ultimately, however, the navy's role at Guantanamo expanded, especially during and after construction of the Panama Canal. It, too, needed protection—a matter that seemingly became acute when the United States entered WWI in 1917.

During the 1920s, the United States routinely intervened militarily in Latin America and the Caribbean. Presumably, the base at Guantanamo was deeply involved in these operations: in Guatemala in 1920; in Panama and Costa Rica in 1921; in Honduras in 1924 and again in 1925; and in Nicaragua in 1926. The Harding and Coolidge administrations, it seems, simply applied the meaning of the Platt amendment to the entire Caribbean basin. The twenties, of course, were years of extraordinary prosperity, and the financial costs of these operations were not especially controversial. The onset of the Great Depression, however, altered perceptions and policy. Hoover wanted to tighten government spending to address the economic crisis; Franklin Roosevelt, pursuing expensive New Deal programs, wanted to find savings wherever he could. Interventionism, or, rather, the abandonment of it, was an obvious way of cutting federal expenses in one area to make other expenditures more affordable. Accordingly, in 1934 FDR announced his Good Neighbor Policy—American military interventionism in neighboring states was at an end. The United States, in effect, abandoned the Platt amendment. It did not, however, abandon Guantanamo. Instead, it entered into a lease agreement with the Cuban government by which the United States agreed to pay several thousand dollars per year to maintain its presence at the base. The rationale—the justification—for remaining at Guantanamo had obviously changed, but to what? The

22. Hansen, *Guantanamo*, 154–55.

answer to that question remained unclear until WWII. German submarines in the Caribbean and their obvious threat to allied shipping and the Panama Canal provided the base a role to play.[23] When the war ended it reverted to what it actually had been throughout the thirties—an expensive installation that endured as a result of "bureaucratic inertia." The base had been there for nearly half a century. Why get rid of it?

In the 1950s, Cuba experienced increasing internal unrest. Insurgency against Fulgencio Batista, an American puppet, grew in intensity until January 1, 1959, when Fidel Castro came to power. Not long afterward, the new leader declared his dedication to communism, and Cuba became a player in the Cold War arena. Both the outgoing Eisenhower and the incoming Kennedy administrations wanted Castro overthrown.[24] Guantanamo actively participated in the Bay of Pigs operation, although to this day many details remain unclear.[25] It was also involved in JFK's Operation Mongoose, an effort to harass and undermine the Castro regime; it aimed to provoke Castro into launching an attack on the naval base, giving the United States justification for marching into Cuba and eliminating the regime.[26] Castro, of course, did not take the bait—not even during the 1962 missile crisis. Nonetheless, Guantanamo basically shed its pretense as a benign presence in the region.[27] Since then, Guantanamo has served mainly as a finger in the eye of the Castro regime. Yet it did have other things to do. In the 1980s, for example, it was deeply involved in stopping the flow of refugees from

23. Ibid., 182.
24. Ibid., 222–24.
25. Ibid., 224–25.
26. Ibid., 226.
27. Ibid., 224–25, 231.

Haiti. It intercepted their small escape boats in the Windward Passage and returned them to their homeland, even though many faced severe retaliation upon their return.[28]

After 9/11, the naval base acquired a new mission—to serve as a prison for Islamic jihadists, including those who took down the Twin Towers as well as those captured during the American counterattack in Afghanistan. Conditions at the detention facility are controversial, but all efforts to close it have failed. Indeed a variety of reasons justify shutting it down. One of them is money, which, in view of our annual budgetary deficits, should carry some weight. In fiscal year 2012, the detention operation cost taxpayers $448.3 million; estimated costs for FY 2013 and FY 2014 were, respectively, $454.1 million and $443.0 million.[29] In fact, from 2002 through 2011, operating the facility cost a staggering $3,896,800,000.[30] This amount was on top of whatever the bill was to support the 5,800 personnel on duty there, their families, and their "Little America" environment.

The day will surely come when the detention center closes down. Then what? If the past serves as a guide, then our leaders in Congress and the executive branch will come up with some new reason to retain the naval base. After all, the "reason" to hold on to the base has shifted several times over the last 115 years: from protecting American investments, to

28. Hansen, *Guantanamo*, chapter 8.
29. Department of Defense, "Guantanamo Bay, Cuba (GTMO), Costs (Detention Operation), attachment to Chuck Hagel, Secretary of Defense to Adam Smith, House Committee on Armed Services, June 27, 2013. This report is available online. Google "Cost of Guantanamo Detention Operations"; navigate to ACLU, "Wasted Opportunities: The Cost of Detention Operations at Guantanamo Bay," scroll to the bottom, and then click no. 5, Secretary of Defense, "Cost of Detention Operations at Guantanamo Bay," 3.
30. Ibid., 3.

guarding the region and the Canal Zone, to defending against possible Nazi submarine attacks, to opposing and making life difficult for the communist Castro regime, to returning Haitian refugees, to imprisoning terrorists. Yet the fact that the rationale for maintaining the base has changed again and again suggests that there really is no good reason to maintain it at all.[31] Closing the detention center will create the opportunity to dispossess the base and return it to the Cuban people. Doing so will complete the process of normalizing Cuban-American relations, which President Obama has undertaken and advanced. We will lose nothing by withdrawing from Guantanamo. As Johnathan Hansen has observed, "Fifty years after Castro's rise to power, Guantanamo's strategic irrelevance is universally recognized."[32]

What will we gain? A lot: better dealings with a near neighbor, the business and commercial benefits that will inevitably flow from an improved relationship, and, last but far from least, huge financial savings that will reduce our annual budgetary deficits. We can easily discern what Andrew Jackson's advice would be: if the deployments cost more than they are worth, then savings to taxpayers are hidden somewhere in the budget and must be found and procured. Waste is a problem that can be solved.

Fortunately, we do not have to stretch our imaginations all the way back to the Age of Jackson for guidance on what to do about our overseas bases that have outlived their purpose. In fact, we do not have to reach back in time any further than the 1970s and the example of Panama. The Nixon and Ford

31. I am grateful to Ariana Colon, my former student, for calling this matter to my attention and making it the focus of her senior thesis, "Guantanamo Naval Base: What Is the Reason for US Occupancy?," Felician University (May 2015). On file at the Felician University Library. 32. Hansen, *Guantanamo*, 356.

administrations undertook negotiations with Panama to return the Panama Canal and the American-held Canal Zone around it to the government there. The effort, recognizing that the United States had acquired "rights" to build and secure a canal at the isthmus under dubious circumstance in 1903, aimed at improving US relations throughout Latin America and, no doubt, cutting expenses. President Jimmy Carter's subsequent support of the project rendered the matter non-partisan, and in September 1977 the United States and Panama signed two treaties. One, the Panama Neutrality Treaty, permitted the United States to defend the canal if it were threatened. The other, the Panama Canal Treaty, required the withdrawal of American forces from Panama and cession of the canal itself to Panama by January 1, 2000. The Senate ratified both treaties in the spring of 1978, and Carter signed the implementation legislation the following year. The process began.[33]

Pulling out of Panama was expensive. Much had to be removed—vehicles, office equipment, military hardware, and a lot more. At the end of FY 1993 the Government Accounting Office reported, with the concurrence of the Department of Defense, that the evacuation had already cost $770 million, with anticipated expenses over the remaining six years to run an additional $554 million. In other words, the withdrawal cost more than a billion dollars.[34] Over the period from 1979–1999, the average yearly cost amounted to $66 million.

33. For an authoritative summary of these matters, see US Department of State, Office of the Historian, Milestones: 1977–1980, "The Panama Canal and the Torrijos-Carter Treaties," https://history.state.gov/milestones/1977-1980/panama-canal.
34. Government Accountability Office report, DOD's Drawdown Plan for the US Military in Panama (August, 1995), appendix I, "Comments from the Department of Defense," 21.

What it had cost to maintain the American presence in Panama before ratification and implementation of the treaties is difficult to ascertain. Ordinarily and for many years the federal government had supported approximately 8,000 troops, their families, and their "little America" lifestyle. Whatever the actual annual cost of all that was, this much is certain: it is no longer being spent, and savings have likely already exceeded the total cost of the withdrawal. Applying the Panama solution to Guantanamo and other outdated installations will go a long way toward closing our annual budget gaps. But that, of course, will require congressional responsibility and discipline.

5

THE PERILS OF PARTISANSHIP

ELIMINATING THE ANNUAL BUDGET DEFICIT IS THE NECESSARY first step to shrink the national debt. Vibrant and consistent economic growth is essential for that purpose. Developing and implementing policies and programs that promote vigorous economic growth must constitute a high national priority, regardless of who serves as president and regardless of which party holds majorities in the House and Senate. But recent history suggests that a non-partisan consensus on what those policies and programs ought to be is probably unachievable. Compromise has become a dirty word, and the national legislature, as a result, suffers paralysis. Nothing important seems to get done—one major reason why the American people collectively hold Congress in extraordinary low esteem. Our two-party system, it seems, no longer works. Yet only a healthy party system (or, as we shall see, a no-party system) can create the policies and programs to secure muscular economic growth.

Yet it is worth remembering that paralyzing partisanship is not peculiar to our era. It has raised its head at various times in our history (in the 1790s and the 1850s, for examples), confirming a possibility that troubled the Founding Fathers. Indeed, those who wrote the Constitution at Philadelphia in 1787 made no provision for political parties in the nation's fundamental law. The reason was that the Founders feared the development of political parties and hoped they would never emerge.[1] James Madison, the reputed "father of the Constitution," addressed this concern in Federalist no. 10.[2] He argued that "in the conflicts of rival parties" the general welfare gets ignored.[3] Why? Because groups with common interests band together to pursue what benefits themselves rather than the common good. The stronger "faction" will dominate affairs at the minority's expense.[4] Political parties permit self-seeking demagogues to pervert republican government and to subvert traditional liberties. Political parties were, in other words, dangerous institutions. Madison, it is important to note, spoke for many of the Founders regarding the perils of partisanship.[5]

Despite the Founders' concerns, political parties emerged rapidly in the decade following the ratification and imple-

1. Richard Hofstadter, *The Idea of a Party System: The Rise of Legitimate Opposition in the United States, 1780–1840* (Berkeley: University of California Press, 1969), 40–73.
2. Clinton Rossiter, ed., *The Federalist Papers* (New York: NAL Penguin, 1961), 77–84.
3. Ibid., 77.
4. Ibid., 79.
5. Hofstadter, *Idea of a Party System*, 40–73.

mentation of the Constitution in 1788. Alexander Hamilton's financial program (the Funding Act of 1790) and the Bank of the United States (1791) exposed fissures within the legislative and executive branches of the government, but it was the foreign-policy crises of the 1790s that caught the attention of the American public and precipitated a party system. The Jeffersonian Republicans, critics of President Washington's neutrality policy, and the Federalists, advocates of maintaining peace between the United States and the former Mother Country, organized and ran candidates for public office. A two-party system characterized American government before George Washington's retirement in 1797. These institutions lacked constitutional authorization. Instead, they functioned extraconstitutionally, just as the Republican and Democratic parties function today.

In 1800 the Jeffersonian Republicans defeated the Federalists, and the latter, observing the constitutional rules, peacefully surrendered power to the victorious opposition, setting an extraordinarily important precedent. Be that as it may, however, antiparty sentiment endured. Conventional wisdom still maintained that factional rivalry undermined the health of republican government. The allegations, accusations, distortions, lies, and shrillness with which Jeffersonians and Federalists attacked each other cast party competition into a life-and-death struggle between good and evil. Each party sought to vanquish the other, to root it out of the body politic, to eliminate it as an institution in American political life.[6] The Manichaean nature of the party division renders Jefferson's now-famous remark in his first inaugural address— "We are all Republicans; we are all Federalists"—both con-

6. Ibid., chapters 2–4.

descending and hypocritical. The truth was that Jefferson would have welcomed the disestablishment and disappearance of the Federalist Party. (The idea that two political parties could coexist and engage in electoral competition for the greater public good had not yet been born.)

Jefferson's wish, and that of the Republican Party, came true after the War of 1812. As president, Jefferson, and then his successor, James Madison, had tried hard to keep the United States out of the Napoleonic Wars by relying on economic sanctions to punish nations that violated American neutral rights. Jefferson's Embargo Act (1807), severing trade with all warring nations, was distinctly unpopular in mercantile New England. Its replacements, the Non-intercourse Act (1809) and Macon's Bill no. 2 (1810) were as unpopular and unsuccessful as the Embargo. In the end, war between the United States and Great Britain broke out in 1812. The former, however, was ill prepared, both financially and militarily, for armed conflict against the former Mother Country. Matters, generally speaking, went badly. In 1814, for example, British forces attacked and burned Washington, DC. The future looked grim, and late that year Federalist leaders gathered at Hartford, Connecticut, to discuss what needed to be done to address the crisis, especially as it bore down on New England. They wound up recommending several constitutional amendments to secure redress from the impact of an unpopular war. Yet those who participated in the Hartford Convention were unaware that an American delegation at Ghent in Belgium had signed a treaty of peace with its British counterpart on Christmas Eve. In addition, of course, they did not know that a week into the New Year Andrew Jackson would decisively defeat a British army at New Orleans. Americans learned of the New Orleans victory first, and afterward the peace signed at Ghent. For many Americans, the chronology of news arrival meant that the United States had won the war, which, of course, was not really the case.

Nonetheless, the Federalist Party suffered an immediate backlash. The Hartford Convention, critical of the war as it was, suggested Federalist disloyalty to the country in its hour of victory. Jeffersonians seized on this perception to discredit the Federalists as traitors. The label stuck, and fewer and fewer Americans subsequently identified themselves as Federalists. The party evaporated. It ran its last presidential candidate in 1816. What followed was a decade of one-party government in American political history.

The fact that only one party governed national affairs from 1816 to 1826 has largely been forgotten, in much the same way that our brief experience of national debt freedom (1835–1837) has escaped our collective memory. In American high school and college history texts the post-Ghent period is often labeled "the era of good feelings," repeating a characterization of the Monroe administrations coined by a journalist in 1817. "Feelings," of course, were "good" because party strife had disappeared from American political culture. (Many Americans may be surprised to learn this because we have been taught that one-party government is the same as dictatorship.) One party had thoroughly vanquished the other. The new faction-free order resembled, at least superficially, the kind of republican regime for which the Founders had hoped. Reflecting the prevailing consensus, Congress in 1817 enacted a redemption measure, which spelled out in specific detail how the United States would discharge its postwar national debt. This law was extraordinarily important because debt freedom constituted a central element of revolutionary-era republicanism, and the law defined the pathway to its achievement.[7] It passed without partisan bickering because there was no opposition. It did not even entail a roll-call vote, and it succeeded. National debt freedom arrived on January 1, 1835. In other words, the Redemption law represented a precise, non-controversial, and well-thought-out plan to extinguish the national debt.

Consensus government lasted ten years. During the so-called "era of good feelings," the Jeffersonian party spawned a neo-Hamiltonian faction that supported federally financed infrastructure projects, a protective tariff, and another Bank of the United States, policies which many Republicans believed were inconsistent with debt freedom. The circumstances surrounding the election of 1824—John Quincy Adams's election by the House of Representatives in 1825, his appointment of Henry Clay as secretary of state, and his programmatic agenda—suggested that Adams was not committed to extinction of the national debt. Opposition to Adams and his supporters emerged quickly and by 1826 manifested itself as an organized political entity: the Democratic Party.[8] The "era of good feelings" was over.

The new two-party system—the National Republicans (soon to become the Whig Party) and the Democrats—quickly espoused dishonest, crude, and shrill rhetoric as the 1828 election drew near. Party victory became more important than the general welfare, or, putting it another way, each party assumed that its views and values corresponded with the national good. (That perspective was presumptuous and remains presumptuous today. No party, after all, has a monopoly on the truth.) Bitter partisanship characterized Jacksonian-era politics. One of the more significant politicos

7. Lane, *A Nation Wholly Free*, chapter 1, 37–38.
8. Ibid., chapter 3.

of that period, Martin Van Buren, embraced the idea that, contrary to the view of the Founders, a competitive two-party system was good for republican government and an increasingly democratic society. Most adult white males had secured the right to vote by the time Andrew Jackson became president; political parties welcomed popular participation in the electoral process and offered the expanded electorate different policy choices. Indeed, since the Age of Jackson we have collectively accepted the idea that a healthy two-party system is vital to our democracy.

Yet the Founders were not entirely wrong in worrying that factionalism could undermine the general welfare. Indeed, our history is littered with partisan measures that sired unintended consequences. In other words, they backfired. Several examples come readily to mind. The 1854 Kansas-Nebraska Act, a Democratic Party measure, resulted not in peaceful westward expansion but in armed conflict in Kansas Territory—"bleeding Kansas"—a violent prelude to the wider Civil War in 1861. Or again, the 1920 refusal of a Republican Senate to accept the Versailles Treaty with Woodrow Wilson's League of Nations promoted instability in the post-WWI international order. Instead of the world becoming "safe for democracy," in the 1920s and 1930s democracy was on the run. One last example: the 1964 Gulf of Tonkin Resolution, passed by a Democratic Congress formally authorizing the president to defend American lives and interests in Southeast Asia became, in the hands of Lyndon Johnson, the moral equivalent of a Declaration of War against North Vietnam. Result: the loss of nearly sixty thousand American lives in a needless conflict.

Partisanship, simply put, sometimes generates disastrous unintended consequences. The cause very often is that a dominant legislative majority, convinced that it has the whole truth and nothing but the truth, fails to think through all the implications of what it enacts. Such was the situation after the United States secured debt freedom in 1835. Debt freedom, of course, meant that surplus revenues deriving mainly from an 1833 compromise tariff measure were filling Treasury Department coffers. But so, too, were revenues from the sale of public lands in the west. The question that arose—what should be done with the surpluses?—should have been anticipated and seriously studied in the years before 1835. Of course, it was not, except Henry Clay's proposed distribution of land sale revenues to the states, a matter that, as we have seen, Jackson vetoed. Debt freedom arrived when the French crisis emerged. Accordingly, one major proposed solution to the surplus question was to spend it down on defense. Once England intervened and secured the peace between the United States and France, that solution became moot.[9] A revised version of Clay's land bill took on new life for a time while sentiment for simply allowing the surplus to accumulate in government accounts in the so-called "pet banks" enjoyed some support.[10] Some in Congress advocated investing the surplus in state bonds.[11] In the end, however, Congress enacted a measure proposed by John C. Calhoun— the Deposit and Distribution Bill of 1836.[12] Enactment followed less than a month's debate in either congressional chamber, even though this was a measure that went to the very heart of the American economy.

What did this law do? Besides creating various new bank regulations, Calhoun's bill distributed all federal surplus rev-

9. Lane, *A Nation Wholly Free*, 175–83.
10. Ibid., 183–91.
11. Ibid., 191.
12. Ibid., 191–94.

enue, regardless if it came from tariff or land sales, to the states as callable loans. Surplus revenue was defined as all funds above $5 million, an amount that Treasury would retain in order to meet all federal expenses. But Calhoun and his supporters assured senators and representatives that the distribution "loans" would never be recalled and that they were, in fact, despite what the law actually said, bloc grants to the states, simple giveaways. This matter came back to haunt the nation in the months ahead, because the states were likely to (and did) deposit the distribution in the same banks that served as depositories for the federal revenues. In other words, the Calhoun bill was inflationary.[13] Accordingly, astute observers began to borrow readily available state bank notes and to buy public land at the lawful price of $1.25 per acre. President Jackson, alarmed that the federal government was ceding its most valuable assets to increasingly cheapened dollars, ultimately handed down the famous Specie Circular of July 1836, requiring that federal land sales be paid for in gold or silver coin. The executive order broke the back of land speculation, drained specie from east to west, induced major bank failures, and ultimately confronted Jackson's presidential successor, Martin Van Buren, with financial collapse. Indeed, the federal government was forced to resume borrowing, and it has been borrowing ever since.[14] It should be noted that John C. Calhoun had had no intention of resuming government indebtedness when he introduced the Deposit and Distribution Bill in May 1836. Yet Calhoun and those who voted for the bill were really more interested in embarrassing Andrew Jackson and scoring points against the president than

13. Ibid., 192–94.
14. Ibid., 194–202.

in promoting the general welfare. The collapse of the economy under Van Buren was very much the result of the embittered partisanship of the Jackson years.

Today's overheated partisanship is reminiscent of the 1830s. Paul Kahan, a scholar of the Jackson era, has summoned our attention to the similarities. "In a hyperpartisan and ideological age, it is worth recalling that failure to compromise and a focus on `beating' one's political opponents rather than governing responsibly has a cost that often exceeds the current election cycle."[15] Uncompromising partisanship can poison even the best of intentions, and since it remains very unlikely that either of our major parties will evaporate as the Federalists did and usher in a new "era of good feelings," finding common ground upon which to build a highway to balanced budgets will be difficult. Sadly, the prospect seems grim, as Thomas L. Friedman has written. "Partisanship is vital to a healthy democracy—but not when it becomes an end in itself, just an engine for politicians to raise more money—without ever daring to stop and challenge their own base when necessary. In Silicon Valley, collaboration is how you build great products with others. In Washington, it's how you destroy your career."[16]

---

15. Paul Kahan, *The Bank War: Andrew Jackson, Nicholas Biddle, and the Fight for American Finance* (Yardley, PA: Westholme Publishing, 2015), 155.
16. Thomas L. Friedman, "None of the Above," *New York Times*, June 17, 2015, A25.

CONCLUSION

THIS BRIEF BOOK HAS AIMED AT IDENTIFYING POSSIBLE methods of narrowing our annual federal budgetary deficits without increasing taxes or slashing safety-net programs. In other words, it very frankly seeks comparatively painless solutions to a chronic financial problem. These suggestions are, admittedly, unorthodox. After all, conservatives maintain that only a thorough revamping of entitlement programs can save us from financial disaster while liberals insist that the wealthiest Americans must pay more in taxes to close the deficit gap.[1] But the conventional wisdom on either side of the political spectrum ignores the historical circumstances that characterized the era leading to our one and only brief

---

1. For a recent and powerful conservative analysis of the debt problem, see Michael D. Tanner, *Going for Broke: Deficits, Debt, and the Entitlement Crisis* (Washington, DC: Cato Institute, 2015).

experience (1835–1837) with national debt freedom: vigorous economic growth; avoidance of intragovernment debt and interest on it; federal investment in the private economy; and paring back foreign-policy obligations to accommodate more closely our revenue realities. In short, ways of dealing with our recurring deficit and growing debt problems that get beyond austerity and tax increases do, in fact, exist. We do not have to choose one or the other or a combination of the two. *This reality is what Americans need to know about the debt issue and to which the book's subtitle refers.* Americans need to know that there are other options. We must be willing to think outside of the proverbial box.

Successful pursuit of unconventional solutions to our deficit and debt issues will, of course, require a degree of congressional discipline to which we are no longer accustomed. Left to their own devices, representatives and senators will likely perpetuate the culture they have created for themselves over the last decade or two—namely, to demonize the other party and paralyze all efforts to reduce the burden of debt confronting the nation unless done on their terms alone. This is a grim prospect because it precludes compromise, without which nothing can get done. Voters, however, can demand and secure a government that actually functions for the common good, and dealing with the budgetary deficits and the accumulating national debt are matters that obviously bear upon the public well-being. After all, every two years the entire House of Representatives and one-third of the Senate are up for reelection. The electorate in every congressional district and in every state possesses the power to terminate the careers of those who seek legislative office for the sake of obstruction. Both parties have their know-nothing naysayers. They do not serve the public interest.

Yet the public interest must be served because, obviously, our future depends upon it. What can genuine interparty cooperation and compromise actually accomplish? First and foremost, they can promote a rate of economic growth that exceeds the current 2.2 percent. The latter falls short of meeting our needs because it virtually matches the current rate of inflation, a circumstance that raises the question of whether any growth is actually occurring at all.[2] But meaningful growth is vital, and as chapter 1 indicated, maximizing economic growth entails maximizing the disposable income of the largest number of families. It provides adrenaline to our consumption-driven economy. Many options are already on the table to improve the financial condition of the greatest number of families. Each merits serious debate, especially with respect to anticipated and unanticipated consequences. Honest interparty discussion should result in effective policy.

What are the economic growth options presently on the table for serious debate? The list, comprised of at least half a dozen items, is well known. Perhaps the highest priority remains infrastructure repair and development, especially in those regions that have lost jobs that are unlikely to return. Rustbelt states like Ohio, Michigan, Wisconsin, and Pennsylvania have seen jobs immigrate to Asia and to Mexico. Only wishful thinking sees them returning. Much the same is true for Appalachia, where environmentalism is menacing coal mining and other industries. Infrastructure efforts in the Midwest and Upper South can put thousands back to work and restore their buying power. Similarly and

---

2. This is a matter for economists to debate. It is mentioned here simply to intimate the complexity of achieving meaningful economic growth in an economy as large as that of the US.

secondly, extending unemployment insurance benefits to those who are still out of work helps protect them from being marginalized as consumers. Their continued buying power benefits the entire economy and therefore helps everyone. Third, increasing the minimum wage does the same thing. It helps the lower middle class and the working poor to remain robust consumers. Fourth, modifying through refinance measures or other methods the interest rate on student loans will free those now entering the workforce from overburden-some expenses that inhibit active consumerism and render the American Dream seemingly impossible to achieve. Fifth, offering assistance to those seeking job retraining upgrades the national workforce and also improves the earning power of those who secure it. Presently, the option most widely con-sidered in this regard entails a special role for community col-leges around the country. Lastly, and most recently presented to Congress, is the expansion of those who qualify for over-time pay, which, of course, directly concerns enhancing dis-posable income. On all these matters room for agreement and disagreement on specifics exists. Ironing out differences on specifics (e.g., what should the national minimum wage be? What should be the interest on student loans? What formula will allow for fair but effective repayment?) is what Congress should be doing in order to revitalize the American economy by generating strong economic growth. The stronger, of course, the better, because it promises a larger slice of the American pie to a greater number of American families. Put another way, vibrant economic growth shrinks income inequality.

What rate of growth will offer more and more families bigger pieces of the American pie? The current rate, men-tioned earlier, is 2.2 percent of GDP. For the sake of simplicity, let's round off our current GDP to $18 trillion. Accordingly, 2.2 percent growth adds approximately $396 billion in new wealth to the economy. This amount, of course, constitutes a lot of money, but it remains smaller than the budget deficits over each of the last five years.[3] On the other hand, if we were to target a growth rate of 3.2 percent and actually achieve it, the increase in GDP would equal approximately $576 billion, an amount exceeding the deficits in 2014, 2015, and likely 2016.[4] One percentage point roughly amounts to $180 billion. Can we improve economic growth by one percent? The answer, of course, is yes. During the 1990s our growth rate was often more than 3.2 percent, and that was not very long ago. If we did it then, we can do it again.[5]

Besides promoting greater economic growth, postponing the interest payments on the money Treasury borrows from Social Security will also narrow the gap between revenues and expenditures, but by how much? One way to estimate the savings is to calculate the average interest payment to OASDI, and to divide that amount by the average budgetary deficit over the same time period. Focusing on the years 2010–2015, average interest to OASDI equaled $105,887,000. Over that same timeframe the average budgetary deficit amounted to $880,679,000.[6] Accordingly, the average interest payment to OASDI, in 2010–2015, constituted 12 percent of the average annual deficit.[7] This suggests that

3. See table 2.3.
4. Ibid.
5. In the 1990s, US economic growth averaged 3.6 percent annually, and in the late '90s at more than 4 percent. See "US Real GDP, Annual Growth Rate, 1990–2015," http://www.statista.com.
6. See table 2.3.
7. Ibid.

postponing the interest on the debt to Social Security will cut the deficit by about 12 percent, but that amount is, at best, just a ball-park guess because the deficits have been shrinking. Whatever the precise amount, however, it will register at more than $10 million, an amount not to be ignored.[8]

Furthermore, as we have seen, an American sovereign wealth fund will generate revenue without raising taxes. Nations with such funds are, for the most part, earning 6 percent on their investments, and there is no reason to believe that the United States would not do as well. Being conservative, however, and estimating only a 5 percent return, an American SWF capitalized at $100 billion would earn $5 billion annually. That amount serves merely as an illustrative example here, and not as a recommendation. How much seed money should capitalize an American SWF is another of those matters that Congress would have to debate and agree on. Congress, after all, controls the national purse, and it would have to appropriate the fund.

Finally, each and every one of our overseas military installations requires careful review. After all, as David Vine has documented, in 2015 the United States maintained "approximately 800 bases" in more than seventy countries.[9] What extraordinary numbers! We have 174 military bases in Germany alone; another 113 in Japan, and 83 more in South Korea.[10] Italy ranks fourth, hosting fifty US military bases.[11] What does this worldwide military presence cost? Defense Department budget materials reveal that our overseas bases cost "at least $71.8 billion every year," but, according to

---

8. Eleven percent of $969,015,000 equals $1,065,930.
9. Vine, *Base Nation*, 3, 6.
10. Ibid., 3.
11. Ibid., 122, 235.

Professor Vine, the true annual expenditure "could easily be in the range of $100 to $120 billion."[12] One need not be cynical to assume that savings—perhaps significant savings—might be found buried in these costs. The multiplicity of bases in Germany, Japan, South Korea, Italy, and elsewhere suggests that redundancies, bureaucratic inertia, and other forms of waste characterize the system. Identifying and eliminating unnecessary expenses are not austerity measures. Rather, they more efficiently and effectively employ our tax dollars. Whatever is not really needed to fulfill our international obligations must be wrung out of the system. The savings will shrink the budgetary deficit.

Reviewing the purpose of each overseas base should not be done only by the defense establishment; the various services, as well as the CIA, NSA, Homeland Security, the National Security Council, and the State Department, would necessarily participate. Yet other perspectives should also be enlisted to evaluate the role of each installation. Historians, economists, political scientists, sociologists, anthropologists, accountants, and others can provide various kinds of expertise that the defense establishment may lack, and which will be valuable to a genuine review process. What was the rationale for establishing a particular base in the first place? Is the base a "relic" from an earlier era? Does the original justification for the base still pertain? Has its mission changed? If so, why? Do other bases serve the same purpose? If mission replication exists, why? Does the cost warrant replication? What precisely are American objectives in Europe? In the Far East? In Africa and Central and South America? These and other questions must be asked of each of our overseas bases in order to ration-

12. Ibid., 9, 322.

alize the entire system and render it more cost-effective. The budgetary benefits will foster our fiscal health, and our fiscal health is a national security matter.

It is, of course, exceedingly difficult to predict or even to "guesstimate" the volume of revenue that will flow into the Treasury as a result of increasing the rate of economic growth to 3.2 percent or more. Nonetheless, one thing is for sure: the amount, whatever it is, is more likely to be in the billions than in the millions and will, accordingly, contribute significantly to deficit reduction. Postponing interest payments on our debts to the Social Security trust fund will also provide significant deficit reduction as will earnings from a well-capitalized sovereign wealth fund. Lastly and obviously, a thorough and objective assessment of our "need" for eight hundred or so military bases around the world and the clustering of so many in a handful of countries could yield billions more in savings. (Success will depend on how honest and how courageous the review process is.) In any event, together these measures will constitute steps toward balancing the federal budget without raising anyone's taxes or slashing entitlement programs.

FURTHER READING

Belohlavek, John M. *"Let the Eagle Soar!": The Foreign Policy of Andrew Jackson.* Lincoln: University of Nebraska Press, 1985.

Chafe, William H. *The Unfinished Journey: America Since World War II.* 6th ed. New York: Oxford University Press, 2007.

Hansen, Jonathan M. *Guantanamo: An American History.* New York: Hill and Wang, 2011.

Hofstadter, Richard. *The Idea of a Party System: The Rise of Legitimate Opposition in the United States, 1780–1840.* Berkeley: University of California Press, 1969.

Kahan, Paul. *The Bank War: Andrew Jackson, Nicholas Biddle, and the Fight for American Finance.* Yardley, PA: Westholme Publishing, 2015.

Lane, Carl. *A Nation Wholly Free: The Elimination of the National Debt in the Age of Jackson.* Yardley, PA: Westholme Publishing, 2014.

Mauro, Paolo, ed. *Chipping Away at Public Debt: Sources of Failure and Keys to Success in Fiscal Adjustment.* Hoboken, NJ: Wiley, 2011.

The Moment of Truth: Report of the National Commission on Fiscal Responsibility and Reform. December 2010.

Nevins, Allan. *The Gateway to History.* Rev. ed. New York: Anchor Books, 1962.

Piketty, Thomas. *Capital in the Twenty-First Century.* Translated by Arthur Goldhammer. Cambridge, MA: Harvard University Press, 2014.

Richardson, James D., ed. *A Compilation of the Messages and Papers of the Presidents, 1789–1897.* 10 vols. Washington, DC, 1896–99.

Rossiter, Clinton, ed. *The Federalist Papers.* New York: NAL Penguin, 1961.

Tanner, Michael D. *Going for Broke: Deficits, Debt, and the Entitlement Crisis.* Washington, DC: Cato Institute, 2015.

Vine, David. *Base Nation: How US Military Bases Abroad Harm America and the World.* New York: Metropolitan Books, 2015.

ACKNOWLEDGMENTS

This book has been in progress for more than two years. It constitutes my first attempt to address a current public policy issue, and I confess that I undertook this challenge with considerable trepidation. After all, history, not public finance, is my field of study. For that reason, I have sometimes felt that I am intruding into territory belonging to others. At the same time, however, I also feel that history should enlighten our approaches to contemporary problems, and my earlier work concerning the achievement of national debt freedom under Andrew Jackson encouraged me to inquire whether his administrations had any guidance to offer with respect to our current debt problem. More specifically, I wondered if the Jacksonian experience in eliminating the debt inherited from the American Revolution, the Louisiana Purchase, and the War of 1812 might suggest ways to transcend the boundaries of the ongoing debate about our current debt—namely, whether to raise taxes, cut entitlements, or do both. The public readership will determine whether I have succeeded.

I have, of course, incurred numerous obligations along the way. First, I thank the Felician University administration and its Faculty Development Committee for their steady support. Sabbatical in the fall 2015 semester made completion of this work possible. I am especially grateful to George Abaunza,

Jaime Cettina, Dolores Henchy, Sylvia McGeary, Robert McParland, Edward Ogle, and Anne Prisco, president of Felician University, all of whom facilitated my efforts in a variety of ways. My departmental colleagues, Sasha Sinkowsky and Maria Vecchio, also merit special thanks for their unbending moral support for my work and for their professional assistance when I underwent emergency surgery in spring 2016.

As always, the staff of the Felician University library—especially Rosalind Bochynski, Elisabeth Gatlin, Mary Lynne Parisi, Susan Wengler, and Mary Zieleniewski—merits my appreciation for facilitating interlibrary loans and other needs that I encountered in bringing this project to fruition. Throughout this endeavor a variety of computer issues arose from time to time, and Alex Iuculano of Felician's IT department came to my rescue again and again. I owe him a hundred thank-yous. I also thank David Vine of the Anthropology Department at American University for email and telephone exchanges regarding our military bases abroad. Similarly, I thank Ariana Colon, a former student, who raised in class and in her senior thesis an interesting and thought-provoking point about our presence in Guantanamo, Cuba, a point which also bears upon other American overseas military installations. In short, she provided me serious food for thought, and I am pleased to acknowledge her here.

I am also obligated to a team of readers who critiqued all or part of the manuscript. Thanks to my friend and former faculty colleague, George Castellitto, for his careful review of the text and his valuable feedback. The same applies to my good friend Dick Gersh, whose commentary has enhanced the substantive quality of the work, and to Tom Chevraux, whose review has saved me from a number of errors. I owe a very special thanks to Nick DeSantis, my brother-in-law, whose careful reading of the manuscript resulted in a long, deep, and challenging conversation concerning my assumptions, methodology, and conclusions. His cross-examination, for want of a better term, compelled me to rethink and to reaffirm the thesis presented here.

A very special thanks goes to Bruce H. Franklin of Westholme Publishing for his confidence in my work, and for his patience and understanding when an accident, putting me in the hospital for surgery and subsequently for physical therapy in the spring of 2016, took me out of action for several weeks. I am also grateful to Trudi Gershenov for her striking cover design and to Alex Kane for his careful copyediting of the manuscript.

Lastly, but very, very far from least, I would like to acknowledge my children—Philip, Elizabeth, and David. Their steadfast encouragement helps get me through projects like this one. My deepest gratitude goes to my wife Carolyn. Without her patience and understanding, this work would not have been undertaken, much less completed; an effort which I hope will help promote a prosperous American future. Because this work deals with our future, it is dedicated to the well-being of the upcoming generation—my grandsons', grandnephew's, and everyone else's as well.

INDEX